THE ZONES OF PROXIMAL EVANGELIZATION

Michael W. Ledoux

University Press of America,® Inc.
Lanham · New York · Oxford

Copyright © 2002 by
University Press of America,® Inc.
4720 Boston Way
Lanham, Maryland 20706
UPA Acquisitions Department (301) 459-3366

12 Hid's Copse Rd.
Cumnor Hill, Oxford OX2 9JJ

ISBN 0-7618-2330-1 (paperback : alk. ppr.)

Ad maiorem Dei gloriam

and the memory of dad

Table of Contents

Preface

Interdisciplinary works may be in vogue in certain areas, but the juxtaposition of evangelization and education has been strangely less popular. This is odd, since so much of educational history is connected with church and religious foundations: the great monasteries, the itinerant movement, Jewish and Islamic scholars. Yet, in today's world of scholarship there is such specificity that those in education, except those in specific programs of religious education, may not think of evangelization as part of their agenda.

The converse is not necessarily true. Those in evangelization have put great stock into programs of education, although, perhaps into its content more than its process. Of course there are those who specialize in types of religious education, such as Thomas Groome at Boston College, who may dedicate their lives to such pursuits. These luminaries of varying degrees of brightness have added greatly to the pedagogical underpinnings of evangelization.

This book is intended for an eclectic audience of educators and evangelizers in the broadest sense of these two words. Certainly, it focuses on two very specific areas: social constructivism and its application to evangelization; and Roman Catholic evangelization. But its purpose is to look at educational thought in terms of the greater good and challenge us to go to the logical conclusion of education, which is the divine. That is, to acknowledge, that bring one to greater knowledge and wisdom is a spiritual act.

To those who are involved directly in evangelization, I hope it poses a challenge to the goals and objectives of what this task involves. To that end I have retraced some of the historical interpretations of the goals of evangelization. Today's interfaith dialogue encourages us to reach out to one another with new understandings and new directions. Perhaps the application of educational theory can help in this undertaking.

The second appendix includes an overview of Franciscan evangelical trends (theological, philosophical and practical). I have included this section to contextualize the applications. Franciscan philosophy and theology have not always been in the mainstream of Church use, but this tradition offers great opportunities for reaching out in dialogue to those with sincere hearts. It has the possibility of reaching "beyond the cloister."

At times this book is light hearted. There are anecdotes and stories that I hope illustrate some of my basic principles. In other areas, the text is rather dry and heavy, attempting to satisfy the theoretical applications of some great thinkers. And, at times, the rather odd combinations of theologians, feminists, conservatives, liberals, radicals and orthodox may leave you wondering.

My hope is that the reader will begin a dialogue of sorts, wondering about the connections among education, evangelization and culture. Whether privately, in a scholarly environment or in a pub somewhere, people's interactions are fundamentally educative and spiritual. To these ends, I offer this work.

Acknowledgements

Even a small book is accomplished only with the help of many others. To this end, I would like to thank the many people who helped with this text. First, I thank the religious order of the Friars Minor, of which I am a member. Their support of the intellectual tradition throughout the centuries has helped to form scholastic thought throughout the world.

As reflective of the scholastic tradition of the Order, Rev. Stephen Romano Almagno, OFM and Rev. Roland Faley, TOR have acted as friends, brothers and mentors. As such, they have helped me in this work and in my pursuit of education and the intellectual tradition in personal way.

I owe gratitude to my colleagues and friends at Neumann College, where I presently teach and Duquesne University, where I received my doctorate and lots of inspiration. There are great thinkers in both these institutions from whom I have learned so much. Special thanks to Gary Shank, Sue Brookhart, Rick McCown, and Connie Moss at Duquesne University. To my IDPEL Cohort and especially Caroline Adams, who had to listen to many of the thoughts in this book for years and helped me to get rid of many of the thoughts not herein contained. Thank you. Nadine McHenry, a great teacher at Neumann College, kept me going with a collegial sense of competition and Thomas Marshall, another Neumann star, kept me swimming in philosophical matter, for which I am grateful. To the administrators and colleagues who were always so supportive of any work: Marguerite O'Beirne, Linda DeCero, and Joe Gillespie, thank you. And, finally to the many students who challenge me continually to be better than I am, many thanks and God bless you .

Introduction

Zones of Evangelical Development

Exactly who needs to be evangelized? We are called to evangelize those who do not know Christ, those who know Christ, those who are far from God, those who know God under different names, and those who even doubt God. How can the same framework be used for all of these situations?

Does a baptized Christian, who attempts to live with love each day need to be evangelized? Is this evangelization process the same as for one who does not know Christ, or God? Is there a different process for those who have always lived in secular society versus those who have lived in a religious setting and have turned from it?

A woman of eighty, a generous and kind woman of faith, attempts to live justly with neighbors and speaks of God in her life, but is unbaptized: Does she need to be "evangelized"? Will I further complicate this question both spiritually and politically if I add that she is Jewish?

Forty hooded men gather around a burning cross proclaiming Jesus as their Lord and Savior and proclaim God's reign and the kingdom of white males. They are convinced of their supremacy and correctness. Do they need to be evangelized?

What about the teenager, who attends Mass each Sunday, belongs to Amnesty International, protests in front of prisons, but has premarital sex with her boyfriend. Does she, also, need evangelization?

If we say yes to each of these, is there nobody who is evangelized? Or does this term necessarily take on degrees of meaning with its very proclamation? Evangelization has become a term so laden with meaning, that it becomes vague. It ranges in description from initial proclamation of the faith message in Jesus Christ to what amounts to the lifelong mystagogical experience of catechesis.

This places Catholics in a difficult position when it comes to offering a sixty-second explanation of the process. We do not agree upon the magic word formula of "Are you saved?" So, we walk gently (and often less than gently) among people of many faiths trying to construct meaning from our own experience of Christ in our lives, the Church that we may have come to believe in, and our relationships in the world.

The history of evangelization is certainly a strange patchwork of processes. The proclamation of Christ has been linked with political agendas, crusades, invasions, torture, and domination. It has also brought with it education, health care, economic development, respect, devotion, and social promotion.

We consider with sorrow the events within the history of evangelization when great numbers of persons were placed in bondage, subjugated, tortured, or killed in order to protect and spread the message of the Gospel. These methods are, thankfully, less popular today, although not without proponents.

In ages past the Church was able to convert large groups of people, even nations to the faith through the conversion of a political or charismatic leader. History shows that when a national leader disagreed with the Church, there were political, as well as, religious consequences to pay. Faithful groups of loyalist could be sent into the fray to help bring the faithful of the land into conformity.

Since the rise of individualism, this model does not work. Large groups, who formerly linked their heritage or ethnicity with membership in a particular church, have moved toward a much more individualized or personal model. We can no longer predict with certainty that an Italian, Irish, or Mexican person will be Catholic. Those countries that were previously considered Catholic or Christian are more and more secular or, at least neutral. These factors are not completely bad. In fact, the Church, herself, proposes separation of Church and state within today's political arenas.

Today, there are many people who are religious yet do no translate this religiosity into membership in a faith community (Gallup, 1997). If people seek spirituality outside of the institution or structure where it typically exists, does this change the form in which evangelization must take place? Are there integrals of proximity toward evangelization? Are people who seek the spiritual, but have no church affiliation, closer to salvation than those who have no spiritual connections? Questions arise as to the reasons people do not choose the institutional or normative source for spirituality. Is it because the Christian message itself is lacking? Are the structures and messengers defective, individually, collectively, historically, or culturally? Do the concepts that are being transmitted lack meaning and clarity? On the other hand, are the criteria for successful evangelization misunderstood?

We must take on a far greater task than in bygone days. We must seek out each individual and find how he or she may be brought closer to the Gospel message. This must be done in concert with the current political and cultural climate of the nations. It must carefully consider the rights of the individual and the movement of the Spirit in each time and place. As a church, it means training people in so many diverse ways, that we may find it difficult to recognize our own expressions of culture and identity within the articulated faith of neophytes or those finding new meaning in the Gospel.

Since the time of Vatican II, we have faced tremendous changes in the way that we view the evangelization process. Simply adding the word process to evangelization shapes a new form and understanding to what evangelization possibly means. The re-establishment of the Rite of Christian Initiation has brought with it new methods and new problems. As we move forward with this process and with so many other developments, we tend to fall into a pattern of programmed instruction, rather than exploring the individual expressions of personal faith. This is, perhaps, because we do not have a means by which to measure, or at least articulate this measure of where a person is moving on the evangelical journey. I believe that this measure between where one is presently, and where one is with the help of another, can be measured. I call this gap the *zone(s) of proximal evangelization*, basing this wording on the work of Lev Vygotsky and other social constructivist educators.

It is my belief that current education theory may help to answer some of the questions posed by this mysterious and mystical challenge to evangelize the world. The meaning-rich world that each of us experiences in our relational framework helps to define the terms for us. Whether we, as Church, are comfortable in accepting a multi-faceted and experiential basis for evangelization, rather than a formulaic expression is a theological question. Since I am not a theologian, but a professional Catholic educator, I will offer my reflections from the perspective of educational experience and learning theory, which, I believe, has many valid and potent lessons for the process of evangelization.

To begin to look at evangelization as through educational theory, there are a number of steps to develop in order to assess any learning task. The first task is to establish the concept, in this case, evangelization. The next step is to define this concept. This is possibly the most difficult step in the process. For this definition, I rely upon church documents and some of the most well known theologians of our time. From this quick review, a functional or working definition will be derived. Many people may disagree with the final definition, but the process can be modified according to the functional definition chosen.

Once the definition is established, we must establish where the person is presently in relation to the concept. If we were to teach political science to a heterogeneous group of people, we would want to know if the members of the group already knew about bicameral legislatures, concurrent resolutions, or the confirmation of judges. It would be a waste of time and learning moments to repeat information already attained. In evangelization, we also need to establish where each person or group stands in relation to the concept. The opening descriptions of the practicing Christian, the devout Jew, the KKK members, and the teenager illustrate, albeit in the extreme, the variety of people whose assessment against the concept of evangelization will certainly vary. Thus, the way in which we evangelize each must also vary.

The motivational factors for each person must also be investigated. What propels each individual to do what he or she decides to do? How will we help to motivate people intrinsically and extrinsically toward the goal concept of evangelization? These factors are both social and personal. They affect individuals and cultures.

Once we have determined the concept, the baseline of each individual against this concept, then we have to move forward with a process of evangelization. This process will include assessing the zones of proximal evangelization, where people are individually and where they stand with the help of others. Once these zones are recognized, the pairing of other learners can take place to help move the evangelization process forward.

Typically, an educator, having defined a concept, would then compare the concept to non-concepts to help strengthen the concept definition. When one defines a verb, often a teacher will then show some nouns to exemplify that they are not verbs. In evangelization, non-concepts are not as clear-cut. Therefore, I have left the section of non-concepts until the end, entitled diseducation or disevangelization because I think it more helpful, in this instance, to follow the positive pattern before reflecting upon the negative possibilities.

Chapter One

What is evangelization?

The Church defines evangelization in the Catechism as: "The proclamation of Christ and his Gospel (Greek: evangelion) by word and testimony of life, in fulfillment of Christ's command." (ICCC, 1994, p. 877). This is a beautiful and profound statement made by the Church. It is succinct and comprehensible. But it raises as many questions as it answers. Are we commanded to proclaim Christ explicitly? What about those who have heard the Gospel message, but, due to scandal or cultural barriers are not able to accept it? Is there a mandate to have people change their religion, if they are seeking God in sincerity? Do people in Islamic lands, where great cultural pressure and limitations to communication can become evangelized without the specific message of the Gospel, but through the testimony of fine Muslim men and women who testify to God's love in their lives? The ultimate question becomes, "Do we specifically need to name Christ in word and action to enter the reign of God?"(I have avoided the words: To be saved, due to the cultural attachments to these words in the US today.)

The document, *On the Unicity and Salvific Universality of Jesus Christ and the Church* states clearly that, "The Church's universal mission is born from the command of Jesus Christ and is fulfilled in the course of centuries in the proclamation of the mystery of God, Father, Son, and Holy Spirit and the mystery of the incarnation of the Son, as saving event for all humanity" (p. 5). Further, it goes on to say that we must avoid relativistic thought and that the saving message of Christ is for all people. But how does this work? In the same way that people respond to different types of motivation, so the manner in which one responds to the Gospels due to the circumstances of one's life is of immense importance. So, then, what must one do to be saved?

The Church herself has answered this in many ways. Salvation is ultimately a free gift from God. The journey in faith and the announcement of this salvation brings new meaning and purpose to life. In absolute term, it therefore makes one better; however salvation is not an immediate consequence for most people. They do not accept Christ, change their lives entirely and die. Instead, it takes years of response to God's call and the living of life to reach this ultimate goal. This does not deny the freely offered gift of Christ or the possibility of immediate and total conversion of mind, heart, soul and action. It simply reflects the reality that for most of us, evangelization is a lifelong process. Evangelization, as a process, brings us nearer to human betterment, as well as the transcendental goal. As Eagan (1995) pointed out, "Paul VI expanded the content of evangelization to include human liberation and development..." (p. 98).

Evangelization Defined

In order to teach a good lesson one must first know about the concept that they will be teaching. Typically, this means that a teacher will choose the concept, let's say sentences, and then define that concept. A sentence is a group of words that expresses a thought, command, or question. It begins with a capital letter and ends with appropriate punctuation. We then try to analyze the concept for component attributes, some of which are detailed in the definition. A sentence has a subject, predicate, nouns, a verb, a capital letter, and a mark of punctuation. Therefore, if I teach punctuation, I know, when it comes time to assess whether or not my students can write a sentence, what it will or should look like.

Evangelization is a concept that needs to be defined. This is an arduous and circuitous task. Since there is not room for a full treatment of this definition in every aspect, I ask you to weave your way through some of these definitions with me, keeping in mind your own prior definitions of this word.

There have been strict or institutional interpretations of evangelization throughout the centuries and there have been broader, less institutional definitions. This section attempts to trace some of these historical and theological interpretations. In doing so, the aim of this section to establish the idea that evangelization is fundamental to human experience. While I will attempt to organize these sections in such a way as to show the effects of culture on evangelization and evangelization on culture, and then lead the reader toward the aforementioned conclusion, there is some messiness and ambiguity in this process. There is mutuality in evangelization's "dialogue" with culture.

The word evangelization has various meanings depending on its historical context. In Church documents evangelization has meant everything from explicit presentation of the Good News for the first time, linked with Baptism, to the continuing catechesis of baptized members, to cultural conversion, to the recognition of attributes in individual or societies that are compatible with the Gospel. It will be my task to give an overview of the practical and historical interpretations of this word.

The *Webster's New World Dictionary*, second edition lists the word evangelize as, "1. to preach the gospel 2. to convert to Christianity" (p. 484). If this is accepted as a basic definition, then the crux of the problem is to define what "the gospel" is and what "conversion to Christianity" entails.

The Church

Mark's account of the Gospel is clear and concise: "And he said to them, 'Go into all the world and preach the Gospel to the whole creation. He who believes and is baptized will be saved; but he who does not believe will be condemned" Mk 16:16 (New Revised Standard Version).

The Gospel account of Luke recounts the commissioning of the apostles, " And he called the twelve together and gave them authority over all demons and to cure diseases, and he sent them out to preach the kingdom of God and to heal " Lk 9:1-2. Matthew's commissioning is more detailed: "Go therefore, and make disciples of all nations, baptizing them in the name of the Father, and of the Son and of the Holy Spirit, and teaching them to obey everything that I have commanded you. And remember, I am with you always, to the end of the age" Mt 28:16-20.

In all of these accounts, there is an imperative to send the message forth. There is a call for a specific action. This action, Baptism, has been an explicit mark of evangelization for centuries.

Baptism and entry into the Church community are the intended products of evangelization. Yet, these elements are not ends in themselves. The true product of evangelization is salvation. The question, therefore, arises: can one find salvation without baptism and thus without Church membership? Once again, I am not asking this question as a theologian, but as an educator. And, I am not asking whether Christ's work was complete or if the Christian revelation is equal or comparable to other religions. My question is far more basic. Taking the most traditional and conservative stance that the Christian revelation is the fullness of inspired truth, the Church states that:

> Nevertheless, God, who desires to call all people to himself in Christ and to communicate to them the fullness of his revelation and love, does not fail to make himself present in many ways, not only to individuals, but also to entire peoples through their spiritual riches, of which their religions are the main and essential expression even when they contain "gaps, insufficiencies and errors."
> (Dominus Jesus, p. 17)

This is still, a very ample statement that allows for religious expression beyond what the Catholic and Christian traditions have often stated. Let us remind ourselves of some of the views of the Church in the past.

Origen and St. Cyprian formulated the phrase "extra ecclesiam nulla salus": outside of the church there is no salvation. Many theologians throughout the centuries have uttered this phrase. Each time new interpretations have taken place.

The idea of a generous God who would allow salvation to those in other communities or other situations is not a modern one. In the recreation of the world of a sixteenth century miller, Carlo Ginsburg illustrates the thoughts of this time period. Menocchio, an accused heretic of the inquisition, expounds upon his cosmogony to friends and acquaintances. His interpretation allows for salvation through other faiths. This view of salvation is, therefore, not new. However, in sixteenth century Europe, individual interpretation of theological ideas was not encouraged. Menocchio's interpretation did not meet with the approval of the Holy Office; he was imprisoned for heresy.

The interpretation of salvation outside the Church has not found universal acceptance by any means. As recently as the 1950's, the famous Jesuit Fr. Leonard Feeney was condemned for his interpretation that outside of the Roman Catholic Church there is no salvation, with its added emphasis on the Roman Church and denial of baptism of desire, an ironic twist that caused excommunication for him and his followers.

> When Feeney was old, some church authorities out of sorrow for him let him be reconciled to the Church. As part of the unfortunate looseness we se [sic.] so often today, they did not demand that he recant. Therefore, he did not. As a result, some former followers of his came back to the Church. Others even today insist that the lack of a recantation meant Feeney had been right all along. Of course not. (Most, 1995)

According to the *New Catholic Encyclopedia*, interpretations of this phrase have taken on three general understandings. The strictest interpretation, such as Fr. Feeney's, states that unless one is a formal member of the Catholic Church one cannot be saved.

The second interpretation is the broadest, possibly not as encompassing as that of Menocchio, but simply requiring some adhesion to Christ (in an invisible church) or adhesion to Christ in any Christian church. Mainline Protestant churches most commonly hold this interpretation.

> Finally, there in the third interpretation that has been accepted by the church since the time of the Second Vatican Council. Formal and actual membership in the Catholic Church is necessary for salvation, for such is the will of Christ. Those, however, who through invincible ignorance are excluded from such membership can nevertheless be saved if they have supernatural faith and are in the state of sanctifying grace: inasmuch as they are vitally united to Christ, they are also united or related to the Mystical Body of Christ. (New Catholic Encyclopedia, 1967, p. 768)

With Vatican II this age-old teaching takes on new subtleties. While it does not change in substance, the shades of gray begin to appear. The interpretations and subtle nuances of words take shape.

The Second Vatican Council document *Gaudium et Spes* states: "She [the Church] also knows that man is constantly worked upon by God's Spirit, and hence can never be altogether indifferent to the problems of religion." (Abbot, 1966, p.240)

> Just as it is in the world's interest to acknowledge the Church as a historical reality, and to recognize her

good influence, so the Church herself knows how
richly she has profited by the history and
development of humanity. Thanks to the experience
of past ages, the progress of the sciences, and the
treasures hidden in various forms of human culture,
the nature of man himself is more clearly revealed
and new roads to truth are opened. These benefits
profit the Church, too, [sic.] For from the beginning
of her history, she has learned to express the message
of Christ with the help of the ideas and terminology
of various peoples, and has tried to clarify it with the
wisdom of philosophers, too. Her purpose has been to
adapt the gospel to the grasp of all as well as to the
needs of the learned, insofar as such was appropriate.
Indeed, this accommodated preaching of the revealed
Word ought to remain the law of all evangelization[46]
[Numbering in original text indicates cross-
referencing to Church Fathers or other sources.]
(Abbot, 1966, p. 246)

Thus it is the accommodated preaching of the Word which must be
addressed by this study. Can the Word be presented to people in
different forms, even forms that may seem secular or antithetical to the
Christian message, yet bring hope, faith, and light? In addition, can the
field of education provide ways in which these messages may be
transmitted or discovered among people and cultures in new ways?

The Decree on the Missionary Activity of the Church helps to
complicate matters. The document begins,

The Church has been divinely sent to all nations that she
might be 'the universal sacrament of salvation.' [1] Acting
out of the innermost requirements of her own catholicity
and in obedience to her founders mandate (cf. Mk 16:16),
she strives to proclaim the gospel to all men.[2] For the
Church was founded upon the apostles, who, following in
the footsteps of Christ, 'preached the message of truth and
begot Churches.[3]' [numbers theirs] (Abbot, 1966, p. 584)

Now, the addition of founding Churches has been added to the
evangelical equation. In addition to preaching the message of Jesus
Christ, the sacraments are included as part of evangelization. "Thus, by
example of her life and by her preaching, by the sacraments and other

means of grace, she can lead them to the faith, the freedom, and the peace of Christ" (Abbot, 1966, p. 590).

The reference to missions reinforces this understanding of the foundation of churches as part of evangelization. "'Missions' is the term usually given to those particular undertakings by which the heralds of the gospel are sent out by the Church and go forth into the whole world to carry out the task of preaching the gospel and planting the Church among peoples or groups who do not yet believe in Christ" (Abbot, 1966, p. 591). There is something of a clarification here, in that this message is directed specifically to those who do not believe in Christ. Another question arises. What does belief in Christ mean? The clearest statement comes in section seven:

> Therefore, all must be converted to Him as He is made known by the church's preaching. All must be incorporated into Him, by baptism, and into the Church, which is His body. For Christ himself "in explicit terms...affirmed the necessity of faith and baptism (cf. Mk.16:16; Jn. 3:5) and thereby affirmed also the necessity of the Church, for through baptism as through a door men enter the Church. Whosoever, therefore, knowing that the Catholic Church was made necessary by God through Jesus Christ, would refuse to enter her or to remain in her could not be saved.[24] [numbering theirs] (Abbot, 1966, p. 593)

The footnote for this paragraph is more specific:

> The ultimate reason for the necessity of missionary activity in favor of non-Christian people is the universality and comprehensiveness of God's plan for mankind's salvation and elevation. Although individual non-Christians can be and are saved without baptism and die in friendship with God, neither unbelievers nor unbelieving nations can live and develop in the fullness of divine life which God has destined for all men in Christ without being incorporated into his Body and becoming one people of God. (Abbot, 1966, p. 593)

The subtle movement is now effected. Individuals may be saved without baptism or the Church, but evangelization helps make manifest God's plan for all peoples and nations.

The document also defines a stage, after accepting Christ, of a transition in faith and morals. "This transition, which brings with it a progressive change of outlook and morals, should manifest itself through its social effects, and should be gradually developed during the time of the catechumenate" (Abbot, 1966, p.600). It is unclear as to whether this differentiation is understood as part of the common usage of the term evangelization.

Most (1995) evaluated the theme of Church membership as necessary for salvation. He reviewed major trends among the first century Church Fathers in the 1984 proceedings of the Catholic Theological Society of America. "We found restrictive texts in Hermas, St. Justin, St. Iraneus, Clement of Alexandria, Origen, St. Cyprian, Lactantius, St. Augustine, St. Cyril of Alexandria, and St. Fulgentius. There are also five Magisterium texts that seem restrictive" (Most, 1995).

In this context restrictive refers to strong demand for actual membership in the Catholic Church to achieve salvation. "We found broad texts much more widely. Only three of the above ten fathers who have restrictive texts lack broad texts: St. Cyprian, Lactantius, and St. Fulgentius. All others, plus many more, do have them" (Most, 1995).

Most summarized his entire study in one short paragraph:

> So we seem to have found the much needed solution: those who follow the Spirit of Christ, the Logos who writes the law on their hearts, are Christians, are members of Christ, are members of His Church. They may lack indeed external adherence; they may never have heard of the Church. Yet, in the substantial sense, without formal adherence they do belong to Christ, to His Church. (Most, 1995)

In response to the restoration of the Easter Ceremonies and the re-establishment of the catechumenate, the "Rite of Christian Initiation of Adults" was introduced in 1972. The text and ritual clearly separate periods of evangelization and acceptance of the gospel.

> There are four continuous periods:
> --the precatechumenate, a time for hearing the first preaching of the Gospel;
> --the catechumenate, set aside for complete catechesis;
> --the period of purification and enlightenment or illumination (Lent) for a more profound spiritual preparation; and
> --the postbaptismal catechesis or mystagogia (Easter season), marked with the new experience of the sacraments and of the Christian community. (ICEL, 1972, p. 22)

Here, in the introduction of the precatechumenate, the text gives an explicit definition of evangelization;

> It is a time of evangelization: in faith and constancy the living God is proclaimed, as is Jesus Christ, whom He sent for the salvation of all men. Thus those who are not yet Christians, their hearts opened by the Holy Spirit, may believe and be freely converted to the Lord. (ICEL, 1972, p. 22)

This very clear distinction speaks of the need to "evangelize" those who are not Christians. Evangelization in this context ends once the individual accepts Christ through Baptism. How does this translate into the evangelization of a nation as referred to in "Ad Gentes"?

The Catechism of the Catholic Church, published in 1994, continues to promote this view of evangelization:

> The transmission of the Christian faith consists primarily in proclaiming Jesus Christ in order to lead others to faith in him. From the beginning, the first disciples burned with the desire to proclaim Christ: 'We cannot but speak of what we have seen and heard.'[11] And they invite people of every era to enter into the joy of their communion with Christ:
> That which was from the beginning, which we have heard, which we have seen with our eyes, which we have looked upon and touched with our hands, concerning the word of life--the life was made manifest, and we saw it, and
> testify to it, and proclaim to you eternal life which was with the Father and was, made manifest to us that which we have seen and heard we proclaim also to you so that you may have fellowship with us; and our fellowship is with the Father and with his Son Jesus Christ. And we are writing this that our joy may be complete .[12]" [numbers theirs] (ICCCC, 1994, p.107)

The necessity of Jesus Christ for salvation is again stated:

> Believing in Jesus Christ and in the One who sent him for our salvation is necessary for obtaining that salvation.[42] [numbers theirs] Since "without faith it is impossible to please [God]" and to attain to fellowship of his sons, therefore without faith no one has ever attained justification, nor will anyone obtain eternal life "but he who endures to the end."[43] [numbers theirs] (ICCCC, 1994, p.44)

The phrase "Outside the Church there is no salvation" repeated by Cyprian and the Church fathers is cause for concern. The Catechism (1994) clarifies the understanding of this phrase for today:

> How are we to understand this affirmation, often repeated by the Church Fathers? [335] [numbers theirs] Reformulated positively, it means that all salvation comes from Christ the Head through the Church which is his body: Basing itself on Scripture and Tradition, the Council teaches that the Church, a pilgrim now on earth, is necessary for salvation; the one Christ is the mediator and the way of salvation; He is present to us in His body which is the Church. He himself explicitly asserted the necessity of faith and baptism, and thereby affirmed at the same time the necessity of the Church which men enter through Baptism as through a door. Hence they could not be saved who, knowing that the Catholic Church was founded as necessary by God through Christ, would refuse either to enter it or remain in it.[336] [numbers theirs]

The Catechism continues by stating that this affirmation is not aimed at those, who through no fault of their own, do not know Christ and his Church. Yet, the mandate to explicitly preach Christ and the Church is stated: "Although in ways known to himself God can lead those who, through no fault of their own, are ignorant of the Gospel, to faith without which it is impossible to please him, the Church still has the obligation and also the sacred right to evangelize" (ICCCC, 1995, p.224).

The Theologians

The Church's definition still leaves much room for interpretations, so I have added this review of some theologian's perspectives. As with every concept, the theologians chosen will tend to skew the interpretation.

> Evangelization, then, is the church proclaiming this message of good news about God's love and his plan of salvation in the person of Jesus Christ. The result of evangelization is planting the church where it had not existed before. In its strictest meaning, evangelization is proclaiming this good news to persons who are *not Christian* [italics his] or who have *not yet heard* [italics his] Jesus' message of salvation. Accordingly, the Catholic Church does not evangelize fellow Christians, for example

the Orthodox, Anglicans, Lutherans and so forth; nor should they evangelize Catholics. (Eagan, 1995, p. 96)

While this definition follows from the documents of the Church, it does not respond to the question of the depth of evangelization. If someone fulfills the criteria of Baptism and Church membership, are they then beyond the need for evangelization? What if the person is nominally Christian, but does not manifest the effects of this evangelization?

> As we have seen Jesus came to this earth to announce the astounding good news: that his father was a God of love and mercy who had a compassionate, personal love for each woman and man, and whose eternal plan was for the divine Word or Son to enter planet earth by becoming human, and for people to worship, love and obey God and to live in love, justice and peace toward each other. (Eagan, 1995, p. 96)

What if a person manifests all of these expressions of the Good News, but is not baptized? Does he or she still need to be evangelized?

Eagan addressed this question in his review of the apostolic exhortation, *Evangelization in the Modern World.* "Paul VI expanded the content of evangelization to include human development and liberation for the 'millions of human beings' condemned to 'remain on the margin of life: famine, chronic disease, illiteracy, poverty, injustices in international relations and especially in commercial exchanges, situations of economic and cultural neocolonialism sometimes as cruel as the old political colonialism'" (Eagan, 1995, p. 98) .

This greatly expands the notions of what is involved in the actual process of evangelization. The expressions of Baptism and establishment of churches still remain, but the fruits of the good news of Christ are defined more clearly.

Eagan (1995) notes:

> The pope identified two groups of "beneficiaries of evangelization": "the immense section of mankind who practices non-Christian religion" and non-believers immersed in secularization and modern atheism (52,53,55); second, the "dechristianized world," that "very large number of baptized people who for the most part have not formally renounced their baptism but who are entirely indifferent to it." (p. 98)

This expanded notion leads the way for an examination of both "sections" of humankind.

Hans Kung, one of the leading theologians of our time, treats numerous topics that surround the question of evangelization. According to Kung,

> Fifty years before the discovery of America the ecumenical council of Florence (1442) unequivocally stated, "The holy Roman Church...firmly believes, confesses, and proclaims that no one outside the Catholic Church, neither heathen nor Jew nor unbeliever nor schismatic will have a share in eternal life, but rather is condemned to the eternal fire prepared for the devil and his angels, unless he joins it [the Catholic Church] before his death. (as cited in Kung (1988) p. 231)

Kung continues to outline the reformulation of the phrase "outside of the Catholic Church there is no salvation" by citing the condemnation of the Jansenists who professed that "outside of the Church there is no grace" and the correction of the aforementioned Fr. Feeney as late as 1952. Referring to the Vatican II Declaration on the Non-Christian churches, Kung quotes, "the Catholic religion rejects nothing of all that which is true and holy in these religions" (as cited in Kung, 1988, p. 232).

From this Kung defines a basis for salvation, and likewise for evangelization, "This means the traditional Catholic position is today no longer the official Catholic position. Even the non-Christian religion can be--since people are, after all, bound to the historical and socially constructed forms of religion--ways to salvation" (Kung, 1988, p. 232). He continues, "As a matter of fact, contemporary theology distinguishes, thanks to this about-face, between the Christian way of salvation--the 'ordinary' way--and the non-Christian way of salvation--the 'extraordinary' way (sometimes, too, between 'the way' and various 'paths')" (Kung, 1988, p. 232).

This view, if accepted, moves the evangelization question along a different road. "No, contempt for other religions is now to be followed by respect for them, neglect is to give way to understanding, proselytizing by study and dialogue" (p. 233) . Catholic theology has taken a great step in responding to the masses of people who are outside the visible structure of the Church, a step, Kung points out, that the World Council of Churches and many mainline churches will not take.

Two other positions are examined by Kung(1988): "Every religion is true. Or, all religions are equally true" (p. 234). These positions are roundly rejected as not including the human capacity for mistakes in transmission and morality. Kung emphatically states that relativism has no place in this conversation.

> No, the reality of the person having the experience in no way guarantees the reality of what he or she experiences. There is a difference between religious and pseudoreligious experiences, and we cannot place magic or the belief in witches, alchemy or naive belief in miracles and all sorts of foolishness on the same level with belief in the existence of God (or the reality of Brahman), in salvation and redemption. (Kung, p. 235)

This reflection leaves us with the question of what fundamental stance the Christian should take in evangelization, redemption, salvation, or in essence, the transmission of truth.
Karl Rahner proposed "anonymous Christianity" :

> For there are men who have been sanctified and redeemed by grace who have never belonged to the Church in an empirical sense, and the reason is that God never denies salvation in his grace to anyone who follows his own conscience, not even when he has not explicitly come to recognize the existence of God. For these men who have been sanctified and saved at an anonymous level, for these redeemed ones (there is no need whatever to use the term" anonymous Christians" if it is found unsatisfactory) the Church is the social and historical sign of salvation, the basic sacrament of that promise which applies to such as these, because she constitutes the visible community of those who acknowledge that in the deed of God salvation is victoriously present for the whole world through the death and resurrection of his Christ. (Rahner, 1976, p.179)

Kung does not accept Rahner's theory of anonymous Christians, because it still assumes superiority a priori. Instead, he sets out the following tenets
in viewing other religions:

> --Instead of indifferentism, for which everything is all the same, somewhat more indifference toward supposed orthodoxy, which makes itself the measure of salvation or

perdition of mankind, and wants to enforce its claim to truth with tools of power and compulsion;

--Instead of relativism, for which there is no absolute, more sense of relativity toward all human establishing of absolutes, which hinder productive co-existence between the different religions, and more sense of relationship, which lets every religion appear in the fabric of its interconnections;

--Instead of syncretism, where everything possible and impossible is mixed and fused together, more will achieve a synthesis in the face of all the denominational and religious antagonisms, which are still exacting a daily price in blood and tears, so that peace may reign between religions, instead of war, and hatred, and strife. (p. 236-237)

The weaving of a fabric begins here. Referring back to the documents of the Second Vatican Council, we can see that there is an understanding that we must value the "light" provided by all religions of the world. The differentiation takes place between the fabric and the threads woven. Less poetically, we have come to the point where it can be stated that the Church calls all to salvation as announced in the Gospel. This good news, open to all people, is culturally, politically, historically, and socially limited. " We want to recognize, respect and appreciate the truth of other conceptions of God, but without relativizing the Christian faith in the true God or reducing it to general truths" (Kung, 1980, p. 587) . Even in places where the Good News can be proclaimed freely, the deficiency of the messengers or of the recipient can impede its force or focus. The truth that may in whole or part be subsumed in the Church may not be the font for every person because of his or her particular situation. The light provided by the other churches of the world can sometimes bring people to salvation more effectively and more fully than the objectively chosen vessel — the Church.

In terms of the evangelical mission we must examine the "ordinary" means of salvation, as well as the extraordinary means where people are called to salvation and redemption. In this combined effort, it is the Church's role to provide the "public relations" of grace, highlighting moments and space where God's grace can be recognized.

Kung raised the ultimate questions regarding evangelization and truth. If we can find truth in some religions, are all equally true? He answered, in part, by way of a traditional story common to Buddhists and Hindus:

> Once upon a time, Buddha relates, a certain king of Benares, desiring to divert himself, gathered together a number of beggars blind from birth and offered a prize to the one who should give him the best account of an elephant. The first beggar who examined the elephant chanced to lay hold of a leg and reported that the elephant was a tree trunk; the second, laying hold of the tail, declared that the elephant was like a rope; another, who seized an ear, insisted that an elephant was like a palm-leaf; an so on. Ordinary teachers who have grasped this or that aspect of the truth quarrel with one another, only Buddha knows the whole truth. (as cited in Kung, 1978, p, 607)

Kung summarized this struggle of religion:

> In both east and west, religion promises to lead men beyond the limits of human subjectivity and the relativity of human history into true reality—that of God or of "Absolute Nothingness." Religion thus claims to provide truth—not merely psychological, subjective or conceptual, abstract, but objective truth, in fact, absolute, ultimate and primary truth. In religion, then, it is the question of *the* [italics his] truth. (Kung, 1978, p. 609)

Evangelization, then, is meant to help to bring people to the fullness of truth. We are cautioned by Kung not to relativize truth or subjugate it. The caution is strengthened in not attempting to "iron out" the differences in religions. Kung pointed to the Indian caste system, the cult of the cow, and superstition and illustrated how it becomes a shadow in light of the Christian view of the human liberation and demythologizing (Kung, 1978, p. 609).

A substantial part of the evangelical task is interiorization. That is, to find truth about God for and within oneself. This does not mean that one is self sufficient in this task, but that one must, ultimately, make this truth his or her own. This task must be both individual and cultural, in order to bring about the marks of the Good News.

So, after having winded our way through this road of interpretations, I have come to this functional definition for evangelization as *leading another toward God*. I am not, in any way, denying the fullness of truth of Christianity or the immense gifts of all religions. Evangelization can be newly established or it can be a further development in a lifelong relationship. Also, by the definition I use here, there is no exclusive leadership. To lead is also to be led. "Followership" is as important an aspect as leadership. There is mutuality in the evangelizer-and the one evangelized. We all learn in the process.

Setting the Goal

Now that the concept of evangelization has been defined functionally, it is simple enough to establish a goal: to lead people to God. Some readers will not agree with definition. Some will suggest that to name God is too confining. It may be better, perhaps, to simply define evangelization as movement toward the transcendent or leading one toward a spirit of super humanity.

Others will take the opposing view. They will state that evangelization, based upon the Gospel, at least entails acceptance of Jesus Christ in some form. Or, still others, may insist that church membership is the goal.

The important aspect here is that, whatever the functional definition one establishes, the goal is based upon this. Therefore, as a Church, we become confused in our application, because our own functional definitions are so varied. In attempting to evaluate whether the "New Evangelization" or the old evangelization has taken root we must review the primary goal of this evangelization.

Chapter Two

How do we measure evangelical progress?

The *Rite of Christian Initiation* is a template for evangelization. It is essentially a process, a journey toward membership in the Church and beyond. The process, in its written expression takes on all of the wisdom and idiosyncrasies of the people who seek entrance into the Church and those who help to lead and instruct those seekers. In the United States, against every admonition of most pastoral theologians and religious educators the process has become a program. It is natural. We like to run programs that fit into a specific time frame and match with our expectations. The problem with this is nobody begins or ends at the same place. People are far messier than this.

New teachers are reminded in classes on methods of teaching, that before they begin instruction, they should list their goals and objectives. The way of writing these objectives changes according to the particular theorist: behavioral, instructional, conceptual, but the essential ingredient remains the same. In order to plan appropriate instruction, you must know what you hope to accomplish. Once this is established, then you can consider the learning population and create learning situations for the students. Otherwise, we find that teachers prepare a series of lessons with no clear image of the cumulative effect or direction.

Programs of evangelization often forget to set goals and objectives, or they set goals and objectives that are the same for all people. The man who walks in, having come from a strong liturgical church background is placed into the same program with the woman who has had no formal church affiliation or practice. This association, as I will describe in detail in later sections, may be an excellent means of education for both. However, one must also consider that in order for both to grow, additional sections for the program must be tailored for each person.

Often the goals that are set are too basic. The goal of the RCIA program is to receive people into the Church on Easter. Yet, if this is the only goal, then there is no need for instruction, we may simply baptize the individual. Underneath the goal statement there are other goals—assessing the candidates' belief, readying the person to become a Christian, understanding and accepting the Creed, setting spiritual priorities for his or her own life, making new entrants into Christians who take responsibility for their own on-going formation. Analyzing these specific goals will help to formulate programs within the process that can address the needs of those entering and those learning from the new members.

Parishes face the same difficulty in each are of their programmatic life. The heterogeneous make-up of parishes means that programs must respond to an immense diversity within the population. Those parishes that have extensive sensitivity and strategic planning have met the needs of a wide range of individuals with great success. Other parishes have met with a sort of success by default. The lack of planning or process analysis has led people to choose other parishes. Thus, the parish becomes more homogenous by default. So, in developing goals, we must know where people are at the beginning of the process.

While I have used the RCIA as the context for this discussion, every action that is defined as evangelization follows the same steps. When a conversation between two individuals occurs in a local coffee house, each member assesses what the other believes and where the conversation can go accordingly. The baseball fan who asks the non-fan what he or she thinks of the Yankees knows informally assesses the situation when one responds with some quip about old New Englanders. The conversation will undoubtedly take a different turn if the respondent complains about the pitching staff or player salaries. The same approach takes place in every evangelical situation.

A group of evangelical, multi-denominational Christians thought that their mission was to "save" gay men. They decided to send pairs or teams of young, attractive, Christian men into gay bars to start conversations with these folks. As the conversation unfolded, one of the gay men who began talking with the two "missionaries" told them that he was a Christian who believed in Jesus Christ as his Lord and Savior. The two evangelizers were caught off guard. Here was a man that fulfilled the goal requirements but was not following through in the way that these two had expected. The conversation became quite bizarre as these three men debated salvation, using the same terminology, but with differing goals and not understanding each other's start points.

While I do not think that most Catholics or mainline Protestants would take on this same task or even assume this cohort of people to be mission territory, it points out an important flaw in the evangelization efforts of many. We assume certain things about people. Whether these people are strong, conservative Christians or liberal humanists, assumption is one of the greatest blocks to effective evangelization. Instead we need to examine where people presently stand in relationship to our evangelical goal. The two "missionaries" to gay people did not really want to find men who were committed to Christ, they were seeking out "known sinners" who could not possibly know God's message. This assumption came back to hit them in the face. The evangelizers were being evangelized.

How do we pre-test our candidates for entrance, our process of evangelization, and our on-going formation in Gospel life? There is a need to assess what people already know if we are to build upon this prior knowledge and expand upon it. No formal test is appropriate. A passing or failing score is certainly antithetical to the process. So what do we do? We listen.

This sounds so trite and dated, but it is the essential ingredient to establishing the place of those to be evangelized. Listen to what they are saying and ask questions about there beliefs. By understanding the levels of confidence in each person or group, we can then help to address the motivational aspects of the group. Refer to the Scriptures. Jesus meets Zaccahaeus along the road. The man is known to be a tax collector, an unacceptable person. Jesus does not say, "Zacchaeus, you need to follow this program in order to find salvation." Instead he invites himself to Zacchaeus' house to listen to where Zacchaeus is of the journey. The people murmur; he is a sinner. Jesus does not accept this conclusion. He listens. When Zacchaeus announces that he gives to the poor and makes amends for any wrongdoing, then Jesus evaluates his standing. (Lk 19).

Take any of the dealings that Jesus has with others: the sons of Zebedee, the Samaritan woman, the rich young man, just to name a few. In no case is one single answer acceptable. Jesus has a good idea of what the situation is in which these people find themselves, but he does not assume. Rather, through listening and questioning Jesus establishes a process of continual conversion. The sons of Zebedee are questioned about their ability to withstand suffering, then challenged. The Samaritan women is questioned about her husband, then given a new goal—to sin no more. To the rich young man, he poses a challenge after assessing his standing according to the commandments. Each response, every set of goals or objectives, relies upon the prior experience of the person or group.

The Acts of the Apostles relates a similar understanding to the prior experience in setting a goal for evangelization. Chapter 19 tells of Paul in Ephesus. "There he found some disciples to whom he put the question, "Did you receive the Holy Spirit when you became believers?" Paul is assessing the prior experience of the disciples. "They answered, 'We have not so much as heard that there was a Holy Spirit." Any pastoral planner then knows where to begin. And so Paul continues with the next step in the process of evangelization.

Paul also demonstrates the setting of objectives according to prior experience in Athens. Here he is surrounded by what he terms idols. He encounters a group of citizens and remarks on their holiness, even establishing an altar to an unknown God (Acts 17:22 ff). He uses this experience, assessing that they are a religious people and builds upon it. A very different objective from that process established for those disciples that have to experience the Holy Spirit.

The steps of this process are fairly simple. We must set objectives in evangelization according to the assessment of each individual or group. In order to arrive at this process an assessment of the subject's prior knowledge or experience must be made. The assessment process does not have to be formal. It can simply be a casual conversation in which questions help to establish the appropriate next step for evangelization. As we continue to listen, we continue to understand what motivators will be most effective in establishing a process of evangelization. The process is extremely sentient. The educator/evangelizer must look at the individual and the social environment surrounding the individual. What symbols evoke a response in the individual? What social environmental situations are important to him or her? While the church may no longer live in a world where one leader brings an entire tribe or nation to the faith, one person does bring friends, neighbors, spouses, and families. What are the social motivational factors that impact the individual?

Chapter Three

Motivation

Antigua, Guatemala-An old man with a week of stubble on his face, tattered clothes on his body, the smell of tortillas and a wood fire about him, comes to me and asks, "Padre, is there a difference between the Jesus of history and the Christ of the Resurrection?" I stop in amazement, pondering the question. A theologian may have answered; the educator wants to know how the question arises. This man, who cannot read, is asking a question that has been raised by great theologians. "Why do you ask this question?" I replied. "Because, Padre, during Holy Week, we do not call him the 'Cristo' until the passion." He went on to speak of the processions of Holy Week, famous throughout the world, of the "andas" or heavy floats that are carried by hundreds of people at a time with their representations of scenes from the passion. His experience of image and story had brought him to a lofty question, albeit one of concern by both theologians and hierarchy with differing explanations.

How did this man's experience build in such a way, that his catechetical knowledge was far more advanced then his formal education would warrant? The Spanish missionaries, obviously, were able to make use of signs and symbols in a way that each person was able to take from them a message equivalent to his or her own faith experience and beyond their formal educational experience.

This experience is not unique to either the Church or this cultural expression. As a novice in a predominantly Italian parish, I watched, as Mrs. Longo, dressed in black dress, black veil, black stockings and shoes, would move from one image of the Blessed Mother to the next. This church was replete with images: Our Lady of Mt. Carmel, Madonna de la Civita, Madonna Del Carmine, Our Lady Help of Christians, Madonna del Campo as so on. There were upwards of ten images, each with a corresponding bank of electric vigil lights. My arrogance was taking hold when I thought to ask the woman, "Signora, why do you go from statue to statue?" attempting to point out the redundancy of the action. "Oh, Brother, she whispered, each of these statues came from a different place in Italy with the group of people who came to this church. There are the people from the farms (campo) and the city (civita); there are those who called Help of Christians their patron and Mt. Carmel theirs. So, I walk from statue to statue remembering each of the communities that are part of the whole." I was humbled and awestruck. It would be years until I understood what she was saying, and probably still do not comprehend the depth of this message.

The power of art is beyond explanation, whether in Central America, Pittsburgh, or Washington, DC. The historic murals of the US Capitol rotunda, for instance, presents scenes of history from a traditional white male perspective. Each perceiver takes from these scenes a different experience according to his or her particular experiential perspective. The middle age white male may see the history of the textbooks of his youth, reinforcing a perspective of right order and domination. The African American may walk away, rejecting the lack of history, invisibility, fragmentation, or selective imagery and history portrayed. The Latino male may hope to find some history as he looks at statues throughout the halls. Finding Juniper Serra may delight or anger him, depending upon his roots, history, or cultural experience. Then there are those, who will walk away bored, never engaged by the art at all, but still with a story that brought them to the place.

Not every experience beckons to people the same way. For many tourists, the *andas* of Guatemala are simply awesome representations of a culture other than their own. For me, the multiplicity of Blessed Mothers caused me anguish and frustration. The Capitol rotunda experience may be just another day or a great lesson in a variety of expressions of culture. In the same way, listen to the experience of people who are joining the Church. Many speak poetically, almost mystically, about the Eucharist or the worshipping assembly. Ask many teenagers who have experienced this same Church since youth and they may tell you of their boredom. How can this be possible?

The consistent element within these stories is that something was able to move the individual or group from one feeling, thought, or action to another. In the case of the campesino, he was moved to a question that brought about greater theological knowledge. Mrs. Longo passed on a bit of ecclesiology that she learned from the authoring communities attached to the statues, and I learned from her. The visitors to the Capitol art displays responded to the affective dimensions of the art and the historic portrayals represented. This affect sense attracted, repelled, or did not move them.

Each of these cases is distinct. They do not necessarily lead people to an equivalent experience or a position of ecclesial inclusion. They do, however, lead them to respond given a particular encounter with another object, person or situation. Since we already know that different people respond differently to different stimuli, is there a way for us to view evangelization as having the same goal with extremely different means of achieving this goal? It is easy to respond affirmatively to this question. It becomes more difficult to develop processes, social situations, and cultural elements that will help people to move. I hesitate to introduce the word forward, because one may presume a particular direction. Instead, what are the stimuli and motivational factors that allow people to change from the thought position they presently have to another?

There are many ways in which people are motivated depending upon the theory to which one ascribes. The behaviorist looks at reinforcement and punishment patterns. The cognitive approach looks at the belief system of success or failure in an area. The humanist divides the lines according to biological and psychological factors. Social learning theorists evaluate expectations of achievement and the valuing of the goal.

The most obvious motivational factors ones are the biological motivators: food, shelter, medical attention, sex, social inclusion, and the various secondary and tertiary items that provide these biological possibilities such as money, praise, or power. While we may not equate these motivators with evangelization, it was not so long ago that these motivational factors were well within the toolbox of the evangelizer. Excommunication was thought to be a remedy for error. People were excluded from the very life of society and the possibility of biological sustenance if they remained within a particular group of "wrong thinkers". The condemned heretic was excluded, not only from the Eucharist, but also from the many functions of society.

More recently, anyone who lived in a strongly ethnic US family may have found that being in a position that was against the church, such as divorce or becoming pregnant outside of marriage, caused them to be alienated from the social life of the community. While these individuals may not have been starved or deprived of shelter, the types of food, shelter and social contact could change drastically. They followed church teaching because of strong extrinsic motivational forces.

It would be wrong to portray this as only a "church thing." Members of strong ethnic groups, religious or secular, have motivational strategies built within the social aspects of their groupings in order to help them survive. Quickly, our minds can think of the stories of Jews, Italians, Irish, or Amish. But just as quickly we should remember the communal exclusion of suspected communists during the McCarthy era or Vietnam draft dodgers in the sixties in the United States. Local civic groups have their own strong motivational forces to keep members thinking within the same lines. The Elks, Rotary, or other groups can be a source of business and political clout or they can help to alienate people through social interaction and informal communication.

Still today, groups exist, who provide food, medicine, shelter, or educational opportunities for those who become members of the group or church. While Catholics have formally moved away from this form of evangelization, there are some who still link the numerous religious vocations in developing nations to the biological improvements brought my their particular vocational choice. Less cynically, there is an obvious connection between biological motivation and the professional clergy of any church. They depend upon this work for their own support. Even St. Paul claimed this right to support from the work of the Gospel.

Biological factors are not the only motivators. Power and position also play an important role. Often these words take on a negative connotation when power and position are used to the exclusion of others. Here I use them in a neutral manner, because they can include or exclude people. Think for a moment of the many roles that are available in the church.

As a young Catholic child one of the first exclusionary experiences that I can remember was not being able to walk up to Communion with the older kids. This was not a negative practice, rather it was a brilliant motivational tool to help me to prepare so that I, too, could become a member of the community, one who could walk up and receive the Body and Blood. It was a mystical time. The motivation was so strong because so many other motivators surrounded it. At that time we wore white robes with blue capes (the Superman connection was another motivator that I am sure was unintentional on the part of the Church), the girls wore white dresses, everyone came and photographed us, there was a party, and we got cards with money. While, this was not as extensive an endeavor as "the collection" of Frank McCort's telling in *Angela's Ashes*, there was a strong extrinsic motivation to receive First Holy Communion.

Immediately following this momentous occasion, the opportunity arose to become an altar server. In 1967 at my home parish, this was no simple ordeal. There were sixty-seven altar servers when I first began my career. We spent the first six Saturday mornings in training, which included everything from prayers to fingernail inspection. Then, on the last morning, we got to try on cassocks and surplices; it was a great day. The fact that we would then have to take them home to be laundered may not have provided the same motivation for mom, but it was a sure-fire motivator for those of us in the neighborhood.

The social motivation continued: once you served for six weeks of daily Mass at 7AM you got to serve a Sunday Mass. Here relatives would come to watch you serve. Faithful parishioners would come up to you and tell you what a reverent image you presented and slipped you a couple of dollars. The real motivator came, though, when you got to serve funerals. Better than the ten dollars you got for a wedding, the funeral meant that you got to miss school. All of these things added up to a way to include young males (the service to the altar was not yet integrated in my youth) in the service community of the Church.

Altar servers are hardly the only members of the church receiving motivation for their service. Think of the many groups within the Church. The Knights of Columbus with their flashy swords (in use only in some dioceses today), the plumbed hats, and capes, the choirs robed or unrobed, who are separated according to special areas. Even the ushers, whose very posture and severity have avoided the feminist challenge beyond most other ministries, have a certain prestige in their service.

Men and women religious cringe when they think of newcomers becoming attracted to their congregation because of external garb. Yet, with or without habits, there is prestige and social motivational factors that help to recruit entrants. One may argue that this is an area more motivational factors need to be included. In fact, it may be because we have been so successful in our goal and motivational orientation toward lay inclusion that religious congregations are in decline.

Everyone likes to feel special. It is an important psychological aspect for all people. The motivators exemplified above are all positive manifestations of inclusion tactics. They become negative, even harmful, if the prestige or privilege linked to these motivators results in the exclusion of others or if they deny the internal reality or sincerity that is supposed to accompany each. I hesitate to impugn any person or group with an example, but we can all call to mind the well-attired person of stature who forgets why she or he is dressed with the regalia in the first place, be it clergy, civil, or family groupings. These folks become the whitened sepulchers that Jesus talks about so forcefully in the Gospels.

Some sources of motivation are thought to be nobler than other forms. A person does not act because of some biological need or because of some form of prestige or inclusion, but because it is the right thing to do, or because it gives the person energy in doing it. The sense of duty and pride, serving your country, making the bed, going to church because you want to praise God, or not sinning "not because of the loss of heaven or the pains of hell (external), but, because they offend Thee, O God..." Many an altar server leaves after a few weeks, because the external motivation of a robe and playing with melted wax and sneaking Mass wine wears off. Others will stay because they feel that they may truly serve God in a special way through the ministry they perform. Each individual and group somehow finds a motivational perspective within themselves to continue to so what they want to do.

These extrinsic motivational factors are not limited to Catholic actions or events. I use these expressions because they are the ones with which I am most familiar. People of other faiths, I am sure, can replace my altar service example with choir participation, serving as deacon or working with a youth group. The vocabulary and expressions may change, but the experiences are equivalent in churches, mosques, synagogues, and temples. Secular society is replete with similar experiences.

I was recently at a gym, which is the perfect example of the multiple forms of motivation. Being a man in his early forties, whose view of exercise was walking into the fast food restaurant, rather than driving through, I was hesitant to join. Athletically, I have always flopped. While not significantly overweight, I was sure that I would be the laughing stock of the gym. So, I mustered all my courage and joined. To my surprise, I was in the best shame of the fifty or so members present. Then again, it was midday and I was the only one under seventy or less than forty pounds overweight. In this world, these were the ones who were primarily motivated by health factors. Doctors told these people to loose weight or die. Later in the day, the younger, fitter people came in, who would work out, mostly, I judge, because it got them many positive comments from others. Whether because of health threat or comments on their beauty, these were the socially motivated.

There are also present at health clubs, those who simple go because it is good to stay fit. While there is the motivator of feeling better, they do it, because they know that it is right, it helps them emotionally, spiritually, and mentally. They are motivated to stay in shape.

Every venue includes people who are doing things for different reasons. Whether it is church or washing the car, people do activities for different reasons. This also illustrates, I hope, that activity and motivation are intimately connected. So connected, that it is hard to tell which motivator is at work at which time.

The social and biological motivational factors are easy to identify in some cases; however, they do not always represent the fullest picture of human activity. Social learning theory perspectives on integrating people's goals and expectations and the possibility of reaching these goals helps to fill in the gaps in the process.

An undergraduate came to my office and explained that he was not going to (Catholic) church because they thought him evil. In colorful language he explained that his views and activities were not consistent with Church teaching and so, "Catholics would think he was just evil." Conversely, he had spent the summer working at an Episcopal camp. His assessment of the Episcopal Church was, "They welcomed me with open arms. I was a saint to them." While this young man's assessment of his membership in either church may not be accurate according to officials in the church, he was exhibiting his belief in reaching the goals and being successful in this group. He believed that he was never going to be a "good Catholic" but that he was already a good "protestant" using his vocabulary. This is not to suggest that this young man is correct, or that his motivation should not be challenged. It is an example of how perception and motivation come together in the evangelical process. Why do people believe what they believe?

This example is commonplace. Think of the many divorced and remarried Catholics who leave the Catholic Church because they do not think that they can be successful Catholics. Some leave church completely. They believe that their life and choices are inconsistent with membership and therefore, they can never be successful Catholics. Others seek membership in a church that will accept their status. They find a situation in which they can become successful.

Heaven and Hell were once excellent motivators for evangelization and "good behavior." The flames of hell, the suffering souls of purgatory, the image of the father God ready to cast the sinner into the waiting arms of Satan for transgressing even the most minor of Church commands was effective for centuries. Once again, however, the Church has been so successful in the cultural educational efforts it has fostered, that people do not view sin and the consequences thereof with the same fear. We have motivated people to believe in a more forgiving and loving God. No everyone in our churches is happy with this success.

As members of a church community, evangelization must investigate what motivational factors are at work within the individual, community, and culture surrounding the evangelical process. The documents of the Church respect these cultural motivational factors and acknowledge that there are elements that may hinder the delivery of the message of the Gospel or its acceptance because of these cultural motivational factors.

Individually, this becomes more complicated, because of the web of motivational factors that make up the individual in society. As we ask people about their stories, we must become attuned to listening to their patterns of motivation. What makes them successful? As we listen, we must also divorce ourselves from the immediate judgement of these motivational factors. The claims, "I am coming to the Church because I fell that it has the fullness of truth" versus "I am joining because my spouse is a member" may seem very different. Motivationally, each person may simply be saying that he or she is able to be more successful in fulfilling his or her goal within this community.

The Holy Spirit, the great motivator in bringing people to God, is missing from this discussion. This is not only because the Spirit is so difficult to discern but also because the role of the Spirit leads to other, greater theological questions that I am not prepared to tackle. If one says that the Holy Spirit led them from secular humanism to Catholicism, the Catholics among us will certainly affirm the Spirit's work. However, if a practicing Catholic claims that she is called by the Spirit to be ordained and, therefore, is joining the Episcopal Church, are we as ready to accept this as a move of the Spirit? The motivational forces that I am examining are the ways that both humans and the Spirit utilize in order to affect change. Some discussion of this "directionality" will take place in later chapters.

Chapter Four

The Zones of Proximal Evangelization

If there is a broader view of evangelization, a view that extends beyond church membership or the "are you saved?" question, then it is important to find out where people are in relation to the Gospel and knowing God. Superficially this may seem simple. If the Gospel is going to be the criteria against which we evaluate life, then one simply holds up the Gospel against each person and one can tell if that person is living a life worthy of this Gospel. But we all know that it does not work that easily, no matter what functional definition one uses.

Even when the criteria set is the teaching of the Church, the individual and the society play such an important role that this system is not adequate. What is needed is a way of looking at people within their cultural context and evaluating where to move next. That is, finding where a person is presently in his or her relationship with God and where he or she can move with the help of another. This gap between where we stand-alone and where we are with the help of another (and here I mean another person, another thing authored by someone, the Church, a group, or organization) is our *zone of proximal evangelization.* We do not learn alone, we are not evangelized alone, we are part of a broader social community in all that we do. We cannot know God without others.

This is not my theory; I am simply applying a well-known educational theory, of Lev Vygotsky to evangelization. So, let me explain the basic theory in the words of Vygotsky and his followers with some application to evangelization along the way.

Choosing Lev Vygotsky may seem strange to many who know of him. Vygotsky and many of his followers were, after all, Communists. There is little or no trace of religious sentiment in his writings of the writing of his followers. As a Soviet era Communist, one may even find it ironic that I would use his theory to promote religious understanding. But, to twist an old phrase, even Communists sometimes speak the truth. Lev, himself, was Jewish, but there is little evidence that his religious training affected his educational theory, although one hopes that the tradition of centuries is absorbed into one like osmosis, without one even knowing it.

The work of Lev Vygotsky, Michael Cole and other sociocultural or social constructivist psychologists may be used as a basis in addressing the cultural elements of evangelization. Vygotsky's emphasizes that the whole person is of primary importance for discussing the individual as a member of a community or in relation with another. In terms of church or society this is essential. Vygotsky referred to this topic in *Thinking and Speech* [italics his] when he wrote that conscience "...is a complex whole of cognition, motivations, and emotional feelings." (Blanc in Moll, 1990, p. 37)

While Vygotsky outlined the social and cultural dimensions of education through formal examples, it is Cole who develops the concept fully. Recognizing the cultural elements in the evangelical process, especially outside of the formal church process, is not an easy task. "It has long been recognized that culture is very difficult for humans to think about. Like fish in water, we fail to 'see' culture because it is the medium within which we exist. Encounters with other cultures make it easier to grasp our own as an object of thought" (Cole, 1986, p. 80).

"Ultimately, education always denotes an alteration in inherited forms of behavior and a process of fostering new modes of reaction" (Vygotsky, 1997, p. 7). Education must help to transform or change the person. Vygotsky seems to look at the total cultural focus of education. To change a milieu is to change people, which is, also, the role of evangelization. "The psychological nature of the educational process is entirely the same, whether we wish to educate a goon [fascist] or a worker, whether we are training an acrobat or an efficient office worker. Our concerns must be focused only on the very mechanism involved in the formation of new reactions, whatever the ultimate benefits we hope to achieve by these reactions" (Vygotsky, as cited in Cole, 1996, p. 55).

Throughout this work I will interchange Vygotsky's Zones of Proximal Development (ZPD) with my own application of this term to the Zones of Evangelical Development (ZPE). The application to evangelization means that we can start from any position and move forward according to a sociocultural process. The evangelizer becomes, not the storehouse of all knowledge, answering every question about God and the Church, but the guide or manipulator of experiences within a culture in order to help learning take place. This notion would obviously not take away the need for the presentation of information or the explanation of certain processes or algorithms, but it sets in motion an understanding that there is certain relativity to the learning experience created by the learner's experience and culture.

Educational and cultural psychological perspectives on the educational process are group oriented, as are the perspectives on church membership. This understanding of the educational process reveals the absolute need for interpersonal relationship or a stimulus that reflects some interpersonal activity.

> I take the main characteristics of cultural psychology to be as follows: It emphasizes mediated action in context. It insists on the importance of the "genetic method" understood broadly to include historical, ontogenetic, and microgenetic levels of analysis. It seeks to ground its analysis in everyday life events. It assumes that mind emerges in the joint mediated activity of people. Mind, then is in an important sense, "co-constructed" and distributed. It assumes that individuals are active agents in their own development but do not act in settings entirely of their own choosing. It rejects cause-effect, stimulus-response, explanatory science in favor of a science that emphasizes the emergent nature of the mind in activity and that acknowledges a central role for interpretation in its explanatory framework. It draws upon methodologies from the humanities as well as from the social and biological sciences. (Cole, 1997, p. 104)

If we accept Vygotsky's elements of the educational process, then it is not the stimulus alone that is important, but also how people perceive this stimulus. Introducing a dog into the classroom may be perceived by some as enjoyable and exciting, while others may feel in the presence of the animal fear and dread. Within the educational process there are subjective responses to so-called objective stimuli. Each stimulus or motivational catalyst must be analyzed for its resultant perception.

Objectively, one might think that the presence of the character "Big Bird" would evoke peels of delight and foster learning. Some children may perceive this character as overpowering and fearsome. In adult learning too, there is sometimes the assumption that certain elements should be educational. A public broadcasting special on Afghanistan, for instance, is objectively thought more educational than a baseball game. In the analysis, however, the adult may perceive the game as having more educational value. Analysis of the individual and the context and perception in learning must take place.

Education Affects Culture

The manipulation of the environment is necessary for education according to socioculturists. "Thus we arrive at the following formula of the educational process: Education is realized through the student's own experience, which is wholly determined by the environment, and the role of the teacher is then reduced to directing and guiding the environment " (Cole, 1997, p. 50).

The effect of education on the students themselves must be based on a total process of reaction to the following: the perception of stimulation, the processing of the stimulation, and the responding action (Vygotsky, 1997). "From the foregoing, we see that the student's experience, the formation of conditional reflexes, is determined wholly and without exception by the social environment. It is only necessary to change the social environment, and human behavior likewise changes at once (Cole, 1997, p. 48).

As one seeks to manipulate the environment educationally in the micro-sphere of reality, it becomes rapidly apparent that the macrosphere of reality also plays an important role in education. Education can help to shape a culture. Examples of this postulate range from formal education debates to common experience. The historic choice of the King James Bible to be read within public schools led the Catholic Council of Baltimore to establish a system of Catholic Schools in the United States. Educational requirements for voting, the establishment of standards, the teaching of Darwinian evolutionary thought, have all impacted the culture and politics of the nation.

Does culture affect education, education affect culture, or do they affect each other equally? There are many mutualities and tensions involved among these elements. This same interplay will be evident in the cultural applications with evangelization.

When individuals or groups enter into the educational process, a relationship is presumed between the more advanced and the less advanced learner. Traditionally this is spoken of as the student-teacher relationship. In this relationship, there is the supposition that one will impart to the other information or skills that he or she was previously lacking. This additive dimension of the teaching/learning process has usually been seen as a positive addition.

In cultures where education for subgroups has not been valued (women, slaves, lay brothers, peasants), the element of the process that was debated was not the educational process, but the content. Thus, a woman in the United States in the 1800s may not have been encourage to pursue a higher level of formal education, but skill development in domestic tasks or household administration would be valued. In each case the common consensus would be that this addition of skills would make the person more useful, more productive, and thus, more valued.

The Zones of Proximal Development

Within the Vygotskian corpus is the basic concept, already introduced, of the Zones of Proximal Development (ZPD). Vygotsky defined the zones of proximal development (ZPD) as "… the difference between the actual development level as determined by independent problem solving and the level of potential development as determined through problem solving under adult guidance or in collaboration with more capable peers [italics his]" (Vygotsky, 1978, p.85).

The perspective by which one looks at learning differs between the actual and potential levels of the development of the learner. "The actual development level characterizes mental development retrospectively, while the zone of proximal development characterizes mental development prospectively. The zone of proximal development furnishes psychologists and educators with a tool through which the internal course of development can be understood" (Vygotsky, 1978, pp. 86-87).

Galimore and Tharp further dissect the ZPD into its constituent parts:

> Within this definition is the understanding of a more advanced learner (adult or capable peer) and a lesser learner. The more advanced learner helps in the progression through the ZPD in four stages: *"Stage 1: Where performance is assisted by more capable others. Stage 2:*

> *Where performance is assisted by self. Stage 3: Where*
> *performance is developed, automized, and fossilized. Stage*
> *4: Where deautomization of performance leads to recursion*
> *through the zones of proximal development.* [italics theirs]
> (Gallimore and Tharp, as cited in Moll, 1990, pp. 184-185)

While the child-adult dyad is the most commonly described by authors, more capable peers can also be responsible for the fostering of movement along the ZPD, (McCown, Driscoll & Roop, 1996; Moll & Greenberg, 1990; Tudge, 1990; Vygotsky, 1978). The more capable peer explanation allows for other students, playmates, siblings, or a variety of others into the developmental process.

The dyadic development is also challenged. McNamee (1990) states, "Vygotsky's theory of development leads researchers to examine systems change: changes in thinking among people as a function of shared group life, not just dyadic interactions that might facilitate change in an individual's thinking" (p. 288).

This is expanded further to include cultural settings as providing ZPD.

> The ZPD can be constructed not only by the purposeful
> efforts of the instructor of the child, but also by cultural
> structuring of the environment in such ways that the
> developing child at any time is guided by his/her
> environment to make use of the parts of that environment
> that are currently within the ZPD....not only instruction but
> also the individual learner can define the ZPD, given the
> culturally structured life environment that provided the
> "stimulus means" for the child's own construction of the
> ZPD and, by that, of the child's own future development.
> (Valsiner, 1988, p. 147, as cited in Moll & Greenberg, p.
> 327)

Therefore, the ZPD can be developed by the active exercise of a more advanced adult, a more capable peer, or, in a much-expanded sense, the environmental stimuli that can provoke such growth. This leads to the question of whether these ZPD end with childhood or whether they form part of the experience of life-long learners.

Gallimore and Tharp (1990) address this question in a cursory manner: "Even for adults, the effort to recall a forgotten piece of information can be aided by the helpful assistance of another, so that the total self-regulated and other-regulated components of the performance once again resembles commonplace shared functioning of parent and child" (p. 187). While not specifying adult learning, Moll and Greensburg (1990) note that ZPD occur within a regular household experience and so are not limited to formal educational settings. "These household zones are also adaptive in that they are organized in many ways, often diffuse, and involve multiple persons" (p. 326). Thus, the ZPD can be found in environments other than schools, can occur with a single parent or teacher, a more capable peer, multiple or diffused partners, or with no live partner at all.

Zones of Proximal Evangelization

At this point, it is time to translate this educational term into an evangelical one. It is certainly consistent with the very definition of church that there is a communal dimension to our life. As a community we address particular needs, work our theological solutions, take certain social stands, and worship together. We become partners in the process of learning and theologizing. There are problems to identify, be it the unfair treatment of minorities, the role of Eucharistic Ministers, or whether or not to have Holy Days. Then, as a church, we work on this problem together. Some may feel that we do not do this to the extent we may wish to or that only the bishops really get to tackle these problems, but the point here, is that it is not done singularly. We know, for instance, from pastoral practice, that there are problems with Holy Days. Part of the mutual discussion is that people do not attend Mass on these days. There is a communication between people, an interpersonal activity, or as Vygotsky would call it an "intersubjectivity". As we establish processes of evangelization and listen to people as to where they are in the journey of evangelization, we are establishing this intersubjectivity in the task of evangelization.

Anyone who teaches, any parent, any human that has begun a conversation realizes that these processes do not occur in a vacuum. They also quickly learn that they are never one-way events. Whether it is conversation in a locker room or a lecture in an amphitheater, there is always interplay between people and other people, and people and their environment. This type of interpersonal dialogue or intersubjectivity, helps us to relate to the world around us and make sense of our environment.

The Church has been extremely good at utilizing elements of intersubjectivity and environment. From long before her inception the greatest mode of intersubjectivty came through story telling. These great stories were passed down through generations, sometimes music were set to them, or rhyme to create songs and poems. In later ages, great pieces of art and stained glass helped to tell the stories of faith to those who were unable to read or may be distracted in the listening.

So how do we go about affecting this intersubjectivity of people and the culture that surround people? How do we evaluate the zones of proximal evangelization in the people who come to us, so that we may help to move this person along in his or her journey? How do we enter into a dialogue with the person, the church, and the culture?

The easiest way to answer these questions is to examine the normative process of evangelization, the Rite of Christian Initiation.

Chapter Five

Zones of Proximal Evangelization and the RCIA

The normative form of evangelization occurs when a person comes to the Church through the preaching of the Gospel or the witness of Christian life. The Rite of Christian Initiation of Adults (RCIA) outlines the normative process of evangelization. In this section, I will examine the normative process of evangelization using sociocultural themes. These themes include the Zones of Proximal Evangelization (ZPE), language acquisition and story. Each of these concepts belongs to the domain of educational psychology and semiotics. The overarching goal here is to examine how the zones apply to evangelization.

In the sections on language acquisition and story I wish to show evidence of how these two expressions of sociocultural theory are paralleled in the evangelization process. Since culture influences both educational theory and evangelization, the connections among evangelization, education theory and culture also appear.

The normative process for entrance into the Roman Catholic community is the Rite of Christian Initiation of Adults (RCIA). This process is ancient in its development. The early Church used this process in varying forms for centuries. Later replaced by more abbreviated formulae, the rite was re-established after Vatican II and mandated for use by the Church. The Rite includes rituals, symbols, and language that easily translate into educational vocabulary. Each stage of development within the RCIA process contains a corresponding assessment for progression to the next step.

The functional definition for this normative form of evangelization is entrance into the Church. The more specific context of this Rite is entrance into the Roman Catholic Church. The astute reader who is aware of the Catholic churches that are in communion with Rome will note that this Rite is not intended for the eastern churches that have their own canons and rites. Thus, while this is the normative form, it is only the so for a part of the Church, even using a strict functional definition.

Clearly, neither the Church nor I assume that a program evangelizes. The RCIA measures faith development in much the same way as ZPD measures cognitive development. It is the individual's response to the message of the Gospel that is evangelization. Further, this process assumes progression according to the pace of the individual. Just as Vygotsky's ZPD builds upon an understanding of development by Piaget, so the RCIA builds upon the awareness that an individual must be ready to enter the RCIA process initially and continuously. One would not place a child of six into a pre-law class and assume that a more advanced learner will have great results in teaching the child law. Similarly, an atheist would not enter the RCIA as a catechumenate with the expected result of immediate transformation. Both cases assume a developmental readiness.

The Rite of Christian Initiation of Adults

The introduction to the Rite of Christian Initiation of Adults (RCIA), (International Commission for English in the Liturgy, [ICEL], 1972) gives the normative form of evangelization under optimal conditions and traditional definitions.

> The rite of Christian initiation described below is for adults.
> They hear the preaching of the mystery of Christ, the Holy
> Spirit opens their hearts, and they freely and knowingly
> seek the living God and enter the path of faith and
> conversion. By God's help, they will be strengthened
> spiritually in their preparation and at the proper time they
> will receive the sacraments fruitfully. (p. 20)

The process of entrance into the Catholic Church proceeds by way of stages. A corresponding rite accompanies each of these stages. The steps of the RCIA process include the pre-catechumenate or period of inquiry, the catechumenate or point of initial conversion, the election, when a catechumen responds of behalf of him or herself, and Baptism, when one receives the sacraments and is joined officially to the Church and mystagogia or the continuing journey in life long conversion.

Using Vygotskian terms, psychologists see inquiry is a time when responses are made to stimuli. A beautiful church is experienced. The responses to this stimulus may range from a condemnation of historical excess in service to an oligarchy, an appreciation of the cultural and artistic dimensions of the structure, a faith response to the church, or any combination of these or other factors. In each case a response of some sort will occur. As someone comes to the Church asking initial questions, he or she is thought to be an inquirer.

The language of the previous paragraph may make the reader question the role of stimulus and response within the Vygotskian framework. These terms are so laden with history that a clarification is in order.

> The Vygotsky-Lurian approach embraces two opposing schools of thought about human development: that which has become known today as the American behaviorist school (stemming from Pavlov's stimulus-response paradigm, whereby the individual is treated primarily as a *passive* [italics his] recipient of information from the environment) and the Cartesian love of reasoning that views "the human mind largely in terms of universal, innate categories and structure," whereby the environment plays a secondary role, "serving merely as a device to trigger certain developmental processes" (Wertsch, 1991, p. 8) (Knox in Golod 1993, p. 3).

It is this sort of mix of response to environmental and cultural stimuli and a goal orientation that is used as a functional definition.

The precatechumenate, then, is the period of movement from the stimulus to the response that entrance into the Church, or at least further information, may be desired. "The first period consists of inquiry by the candidate and evangelization and the precatechumenate on the part of the Church. It ends with the entrance into the order of catechumens" (ICEL, 1973, p. 22). The precatechumen or inquirer looks at his or her actual situation in life. In sociocultural terms, the actual level of progress is the individual's finding him or her self introduced to a stimulus that is requiring a response. The stimulus may have been the hearing of the preached mystery of Christ, as the Rite assumes. It could also be the mediated action of symbols, as one is drawn into a church by the architecture, art, symbol, candles, rituals, or the like. Alternatively, it could be the inspiration of another agent, such a one to whom the individual is betrothed, a friend, or a neighbor. In each case, a mediated activity involves the individual or group connecting with another stimulus or agent.

This initial stage development clearly parallels Vygotsky's ZPD. Vygotsky identifies the Zone of Proximal Development between the point where a person is at the present without assistance and the potential, where a more advanced learner could assist the same person. In this case, the more advanced learner is the community or individual representing the community.

If the inquirer responds with the intention of entering the Church, he or she is then termed a catechumen. At this point, an agent who has helped lead the inquirer to this point or another may be assigned to the candidate on behalf of the community. The RCIA process may identify this person as the "sponsor." In evangelical terms, the cold terminology of stimulus-response would be replaced with more inspiring vocabulary, such as, "The rite of initiation is suited to the spiritual journey of adults, which varies according to the many forms of God's grace, the free cooperation of the individuals, the action of the church, and the circumstances of time and place" (ICEL, p. 21).

A concern arises about the Vygotskian application. Vygotsky usually seeks to identify the less advanced learner as a child. It is in later theorists' work, such as the citations of Cole (1985) that the alternative word "novice" appears. This word has significant meaning in a religious context. A novice is typically a younger member of a religious community. Youth, however, is not the defining factor; it is, rather, the stage of entry for a new member into the community. This very process of inquiry, postulancy, novitiate, and post novitiate formation is based upon the most ancient form of the Rite of Christian Initiation of Adults.

Cole (1985) defines the "more advanced learner" further.

> Here, I would like to treat the idea of the zone of proximal development in terms of its general conception as the structure of joint activity in any context where there are participants who exercise differential responsibility by virtue of differential expertise. (P.155)

To assume that a new member or one who is in the initial stages of entry into the Church through the process of evangelization is not an extreme jump logically, historically, or semantically. Therefore, a new member is partnered from the beginning of the evangelization process with a more advanced learner, the sponsor.

The stimulus to inquiry is another important aspect of this process. The same stimulus applied to many inquirers may not have the same response. Does it then become necessary to reduce the numerous and multifaceted dimensions of stimuli-response in order to examine the way that an inquirer may respond to a stimulus to move forward in the evangelization process? Obviously, visiting a beautiful church, learning about the pope, participating in Stations of the Cross, or viewing the Eucharist for the first time does not necessarily or immediately lead a person to entrance into that community. Multiple dimensions interact to lead someone toward this decision.

There are also numerous goals that may be achieved through Church membership, some more authentic or altruistic than others are. One person may wish to become more intimate with God through relationship in a liturgical community. Another may ascent to this relational experience, but move toward communion with the Church because of the desire to marry another member or to receive a tuition discount at a Catholic school. These goals are not singular or distinct. Educational goals are similarly faceted. Wertsch addresses this by reflecting that "...multiple goals and the complex relationships that exist among them are essential issues to consider when trying to interpret mediated action. A major shortcoming in many accounts of mediated action (including my own in many cases) is that they interpret action as if it was motivated by a single goal" (Wertsch, 1998, p. 34).

Whatever the reasons people decide to enter the church, we are able to look at where they are in their actual situations and their potential situations. Remember, Vygotsky defines the Zone of Proximal Development as "... *the difference between the actual development level as determined by independent problem solving and the level of potential development as determined through problem solving under adult guidance or in collaboration with more capable peers* [italics his]" (Vygotsky, 1978, p.85) . The independent problem solving in this case is, broadly interpreted, as discerning where I, as an individual, stand before God. This is not a simple statement, as its context contains the dimensions and goal orientation already discussed. The potential development comes through the RCIA process as the person, paired with a sponsor (and through the sponsor the community), moves through the steps toward full communion with the Church. This movement is from dependence upon another (one or community) toward the automized response of one's own faith stance, to recursion through the process in further development as a faith member (a more advanced learner) . A more detailed analysis of each stage follows.

Pre-catechumenate

The initial period of inquiry helps someone to develop from his or her actual standing (outside of membership with the church) as an inquirer toward his or her potential as a catechumen. The Church sees the need for a companion (more advanced learner) to be paired with the catechumen to represent the local church and then have him or her accepted by representatives of the community. This reflects the first stage of Vygotsky's progression, where others assist performance. "The inquirer or sympathizer is presented by a friend, and then he is welcomed and received by the priest or by some other appropriate and worthy member of the community" (ICEL, 1973, p. 23). A dyadic relationship (with friend) or a cultural group relationship has now begun in this educational and evangelical process.

In the common experience a person who is other-than-Catholic may become romantically involved with another. As they move toward engagement, the faith stance of the Catholic partner spurs the inquiry of the other. The Catholic partner invites the fiancé to become a member of the Church and brings him or her to the parish priest of RCIA coordinator for further investigation.

The cultural dimensions of the community are manifested within the experience of the inquirer. Not withstanding the important element of grace within the movement or development of the individual, the mediated action of individuals, the hearing of God's Word, and the contact of the community become important stimuli for dynamism. "...the initial conversion and desire to change one's life and to enter into contact with God in Christ; thus the first sense of repentance and the practice of calling on God and praying; and the first experience of the society and spirit of Christians" (ICEL, p. 24).

Using the aforementioned example, frequently it is not the faith of the fiancé alone that inspires the inquirer, but the faith customs and religion of the new family as a subculture that affects greater desire. The relationship becomes multifaceted rather than simply dyadic.

Catechumenate

At the catechumenate, the candidate is paired with another man or woman who will be his or her sponsor. "This sponsor is to be a man or woman who knows the candidate, helps him, and witnesses to his morals, faith, and intention" (ICEL, p. 32). This pairing can be seen in Vygotskian terms as the lesser and the more advanced learner. It will be the responsibility of the sponsor for a period of the initiation to lead the catechumen through the stage of the catechumenate.

This is not simply a dyadic process. While the sponsor carries out the immediate role of responsibility, the Christian community carries out a significant role in the development of the candidate. There is a change in the thinking of the individual because of the shared group life of the community and the individual according to Vygotsky (as cited in MacNamee, 1990).

As a new member comes into the Church, the community challenges his or her views. A candidate who comes from the Anglican tradition may have little difficulty with the ceremonial and hierarchical dimensions of the Roman Church but may have problems with some aspects of papal authority. Through debate, reading, and dialogue the community will attempt to present their belief to the newcomer. As the catechumen moves toward his or her own faith stance, it will be their determination as to whether they can accept these teachings.

The catechumenate ends through the assessment of the individual, the community, and the sponsor. The individual is asked, personally and through his or her sponsor, whether he or she is willing to accept final preparation for the sacraments. The assessment criterion for moving to the next stage is the individual's own discernment and ability to articulate his or her desire to continue to the community.

Likewise, the community and sponsor must testify to their own readiness to accept the new member and to acknowledging the candidate's testimony to readiness. This period may last for several months or several years depending upon the candidate and the community. In terms of sociocultural development, it is dependent upon the proximal development toward the goal of the next step: election.

Election

The next distinct step is the period of election. The basic elements of the second step Vygotskian schema applies. Here, the catechumen moves from reliance upon the faith of the sponsor and community to reliance upon his or her own developing faith. The developmental readiness of this candidate is established through the assessment of the individual, the community, and the sponsor. The rite specifies an assessment:

> Before the election is celebrated, the candidates are expected to have a conversion of mind and morals, a sufficient knowledge of Christian teaching, and a sense of

> faith and charity; a consideration of their worthiness is also required. Later, in the actual celebration of the rite, the manifestation of their intention and the decision of the bishop or his delegate should take place in the presence of the community. It is thus clear that the election, which enjoys such great solemnity, is the turning point in the whole catechumenate. (The Rites, p. 27)

The individual moves from reliance upon the faith of another to specific demonstrable criteria that attest to his or her own faith. While the individual is not yet expected to be fully autimized or completely incorporated into the faith community, the turning point is movement from other to self, which parallels the second step of Vygotsky's ZPD. This new step is introduced through culturally mediated means: rites of election, more intense prayer, the experience of the community, culture, and the responsive language of the elect.

At this point, the catechumen is expressing his or her own faith statements. The spouse who is being introduced to the faith now brings new learning and faith beliefs back to the Catholic spouse and family. Often a catechumen will come home from a class and talk with Catholic family members about a belief or practice such as the rosary. The catechumen is beginning to rely upon self for the acceptance of this practice and yet reminds others of their own beliefs and practices. While the rosary can now be prayed by the catechumen his or herself, others can be accessed for remaining questions, such as, "What is the next Joyful Mystery?"

The Sacraments

The celebration of the sacraments is the next step in the RCIA process. Again, the interplay occurs between the community, the Christian culture and the individual or individuals.

> The sacraments of baptism, confirmation, and the Eucharist are the final stages in which the elect come forward, and with sins forgiven, are admitted into the people of God, and are led by the Holy Spirit into the promised fullness of time and, in the Eucharistic sacrifice and meal, to the banquet of the Kingdom of God. (ICEL, p. 28)

In the rite, the symbolic expression of a transformation takes place. The fullness of communion, represented by confirmation and communion, are external expressions of the newly baptized's (neophyte's) acceptance or fossilization of the practice of the faith, in which he or she solidifies and makes routine their belief system.

Throughout this process, the individual moves from actual to potential development. While the stages, in both Vygotsky and the Rites, are definitive and marked by great clarity, the reality of the individual may be marked with more flux and dynamism. The movement from reliance upon other and reliance upon self may more easily parallel the movement from inquiry to catechumenate in one person, while better represented by the movement from catechumenate to election in another. In each case, one may assess the initiate's ZPE and membership phase by certain events, symbols, and criteria. Through the educative pulling of the sponsor, community, signs and symbols, he or she moves to another zone of development.

As a candidate receives the sacraments, it is the intention that is important. While God's grace remains available and the Church ready, the candidate must willingly and intentionally desire the sacraments. Unresolved questions of faith or practice may remain. The new member may not be comfortable with the intercession of saints, but does not have an obstinate disagreement with the teaching. At this stage, the acceptance of the sacraments he or she is accepting the beliefs in the church in "good faith."

Mystagogia

The final stage for the new initiate is that of mystagogia. This stage is defined as "...a time for deepening the Christian experience, for gaining spiritual fruit, and for entering more closely into the life and unity of the community of the faithful" (ICEL, p. 22). This stage is also significant because, while instruction is a component of all the steps, mystagogia is the time of postbaptismal catechesis. This period, which ends forty days after the reception of the sacraments, is also a time for the community to renew itself and to pass on the teachings specific to the members of the Baptized community. It is, in essence, the period of self-regulation and deautomization for the Christian. No longer totally dependent upon the faith life of the community or the sponsor, the individual is able to stand-alone.

Mystagogia also holds within it another social constructivist tenet, that of lifelong learning. While the formal period of mystagogia ends after forty days, it is the intention of the Church that constant conversion remains a part of the member's understanding of Christian life.

"The time of postbaptismal catechesis is of great importance so that the neophytes, helped by their sponsors, may enter into a closer relationship with the faithful and bring them renewed vision and impetus" (ICEL, p. 31).

The example of the new spouses has provided a context throughout these stages. In mystagogia, the Catholic spouse, family and friends continue to bring the cultural dimensions of the faith to the neophyte. On the anniversary of death of a relative, a family member may invite others to a mass in honor of the deceased. This experience will add to the continued learning and enculturation of the neophyte. Learning in this fashion never ends, for the neophyte or for veteran Christians.

Language Acquisition

Basic to the field of semiotics, semantics, and constructivism is the understanding that signs transfer knowledge. Language, while not the only sign system, is the predominant system for communication.

> The semiotic mediation of practical activity, primarily through speech, transforms humans and creates the possibility of human society. Human labor differs from animal tool use because humans are aware of and plan their actions using historically transmitted and socially created means of production. The awareness and planning ability is a form of generalization made possible only through speech. (Lee, 1985, p. 75)

The evangelization process is normatively exhibited in the RCIA process. The process teaches a new sign system. The new member first learns the vocabulary of the Church in order to articulate his or her faith position. At first, this is a simple introduction to the vocabulary of the Church. The new member then masters this language in the development of inner vocabulary and articulation.

This inner vocabulary is the new sign language that is used to express the understanding of the theological concepts that are being presented and accepted. The beliefs of sin, salvation, hope, grace, transubstantiation, are given a voice in the new member. Just as a child moves from reaching for an apple, understanding that it is good to eat, to asking for an apple, the new member articulates the beliefs that are developing within.

The Word of God as interpreted through more advanced members is explained to the catechumen. In the liturgical setting, the new member comes to the Sunday gathering, but is asked to leave before the recitation of the Creed. It is not until the candidate is able to articulate fully all the truths of the faith held within the Creed that he or she is to recite it publicly to the faith community. In a clear manifestation of language acquisition, the candidate recites the Creed as an expression of his or her own faith.

This language is not limited to expressive or receptive vocabulary. Every action leads toward a greater means of communicating the faith language. The celebration of the scrutinies highlights this action. The scrutinies are a set of rites by which the candidate is questioned about his or her readiness to continue. Optimally, they are celebrated before the congregation with their acceptance acknowledged by some congregational response. The new member must articulate a faith stance each time the rite is celebrated. There is the assumption of progress, although the individual, the sponsor, and the coordinator then assess this progress with the whole congregation. The position of the new member is considered through language development and acquisition.

> To arouse the desire of purification and redemption by Christ, three scrutinies are celebrated: either to teach the catechumens about the mystery of sin, from which the whole world and each person desires to be redeemed, and thus be saved from its present and future effects, or to fill their minds with the meaning of Christ the Redeemer. (ICEL, p. 73)

The new members are being taught the language of the scriptures and the Church; they are being taught a new language. This language is spoken and it is applied through the liturgical celebrations. The catechumens are anointed to show their status as intentional members of the Church. The catechumens are chosen as the elect and sent to the bishop to be "ordered" or listed among the chosen. They are sent away from the gathering to emphasize their own time of learning.

The RCIA process has as its typical goal, the sacraments of initiation at Easter. In the Rites of Easter— baptism, confirmation and Eucharist—the language of membership is then expanded. During the Easter vigil the candidate is again examined in terms of his or her language acquisition:

> N. , What do you ask of God's Church?
> Candidate: Faith.
> Celebrant: What does faith offer you?
> Candidate: Eternal life.

> The celebrant may use other words in asking the candidate
> about his intention and may permit him to answer in his
> own words, for example, after the first question: What do
> you ask? Or what do you desire? For what reason have you
> come?, he may receive such answers as: The grace of
> Christ, or entrance into the Church, or eternal life or other
> suitable responses. The celebrant will adapt his questions to
> the answers. (ICEL, p. 108)

The rite is replete with signs and language that seeks responses
from the candidate that give witness that he or she has an understanding
of the language of the Church and can use that language to
communicate with representatives of the community. Lee (1985) states,
"Language, as a historically determined social institution, is the means
through which society converts the principles of cognitive development
from biological to social dialectical" (p. 75) . He makes this statement
after quoting Vygotsky, "Prior to mastering his own behavior, the child
begins to master his surroundings with the help of speech. This
produces new relations with the environment in addition to the new
organization of behavior itself" (As cited in Lee, 1985, p. 75).

The new member coming to the church has an interest in the
Church and is beginning to formulate the questions about faith.
Through interaction with the Church's language and culture, he or she
acquires a new way to organize thought patterns about faith. Through
the acquisition of language, the candidate is able to newly articulate
questions surrounding the journey of evangelization. These experiences
are expressed in various dimensions. The new member, for example,
learning the term "tabernacle," not only adds to his or her vocabulary,
but also adds to the understanding of the place of reservation for the
Eucharist.

The new member may also finally be able to express to another
member a question about belief or a moral thought for which he or she
earlier lacked vocabulary to articulate the question. The parallel is not
unlike that of a small child attempting to ask for a specific item and
grasping with signs and noises until his or her sign or vocabulary is
finally consistent enough to articulate the desire for a cookie. The
equivalence of these two actions may seem unlikely because of the
content and age difference, however in the action of language
acquisition there is similarity. The new member learns new vocabulary
in the same way as a child. A faith dimension is communicated through
the act of language:

> And many more believed because of his word. They said to
> the woman, "It is no longer because of your words that we
> believe, for we have heard for ourselves, and we know that
> this is indeed the Savior of the world." (Jn. 4:39-42)

Faith and Story

> What, in fact, is gained and what lost when human beings
> make sense of the world by telling stories about it—by
> using the narrative mode of construing reality? The usual
> answer is a kind of doxology delivered in the name of "the
> scientific method": Thou shalt not indulge in self delusion,
> nor utter unverifiable positions, nor commit contradiction,
> nor treat mere history as cause, and so on. (Bruner, 1996,
> p. 130)

The history of evangelization and the means of evangelization are highly influenced by storytelling. Relating the faith story, the great unverifiable narratives help construct meaning and purpose for many people. Stories do not always meet the criteria for proof set by the scientific method. Social science has valued story telling but with has often been uncomfortable with a lack of empirical evidence for the kinds of truth they may convey. Religion has remained steadfast in its proposal that the truths of faith are universal, yet not provable, at least in scientific terms.

Throughout the RCIA program the sacred scriptures, the book of faith stories, is used to strengthen the candidates. The Gospel of John is used during Lent to relate stories of Christ's interaction with others. In each account, as in the Johanine account mentioned above, the person who encounters Jesus is led from a faith based upon a miraculous event or the faith of another to his or her own faith stance. More mature members, describing their faith journey give testimonies. Bruner (1996) suggests nine universals of narrative realities:

- There is a structure of committed time in which the unfolding of events take place. A generic particularity allows particulars to fall within a certain genre.
- Actions have reasons.
- There is some reason, motivated by base belief, for this story.
- A hermeneutic composition is in place whereby there is no single construal and may have multiple meanings.
- The story must also have an implied canonicity, running against what is expected.

- An ambiguity of reference does not allow for a precise checking of facts within the story.
- There is inherent negotiability, which provides a "certain essential contestability."
- A "centrality of trouble" implies that any story worth telling is usually centered upon some trouble.
- Finally, there is an historical extensibility of narrative. There is a sense whereby the story continues to be told and added to. (pp. 131-143)

The evangelical task meets each of the criteria established by Bruner. The stories of faith, both scriptural and personal, exhibit these nine characteristics. The scriptural stories present a structure of time that makes its own history. The debates about evolutionism versus scientific evidence demonstrate the ambiguity of reference and contestability. The stories have particulars. Characters and settings, plots, and genres can capture the imagination and our reality.

The scriptural stories by nature have a hermeneutic composition. Each story, read thousands of times, provides for new meaning in the context of each reader's time and place. Each group or individual can come from a reading of the scripture with an alternative understanding. One can remember well from history class that this very issue was at the heart of the Reformation. The scriptures are so full of meaning that one could justify almost any position from its contents. Bruner's multiple meanings criteria for hermeneutics are readily fulfilled.

The implied canonicity of the scripture is found most profoundly in its faith dimension. Joshua defeats Jericho, David slays Goliath, Christ is put to death, and death is replaced by resurrection. In each case, the story ends in a way other than what would be expected.

Ambiguous reference is a concern among many Christians. In an attempt to make the scriptures not only a book of faith but also a book of fact, Fundamentalists have gone to great lengths at attempting to prove "scientifically" that the scriptures are historically accurate. Using Bruner's "ambiguous reference" criteria, this ambiguity does not run contrary to the truth of the text; it is simply not provable according to the "scientific method." The scriptural references sometimes coincide with secular history and sometimes do not. The purpose in being a universal narrative remains intact.

The centrality of trouble within the Christian scriptures is apparent on every page. Adam and Eve run into a problem with the apple incident, Moses and the Israelites need to get away from Pharaoh, Jesus is born and there's no husband and no room in the inn, Jesus teaches and irritates the hierarchy, Jesus is killed, the disciples are in turmoil,

Jesus is raised, the community fights, and so it goes. Each story within the totality moves the problems through to a conclusion, then to another problem.

Scriptural negotiability may not be a term that theologians or bishops would be comfortable stating. However, there is within the Christian scriptures a certain variation on themes. The exegetical tradition from Origen to the present *Jerome Biblical Commentary* gives witness to the interpretability of scriptures. The field of historical-critical analysis allows for the negotiating of cultural and historical elements of the scriptural narratives.

The very presence of four accounts of the Gospel presented to different audiences in different settings shows the negotiability of the stories. At the baptism of Jesus, does the Holy Spirit appear to Jesus (Mk 1:10), to John the Baptist (Mt 3:16), or all the people present (Lk 3:21-22)? These competing versions take nothing away from the event, but are alternate views of the same event.

The story continues throughout the scriptures. Each scriptural story expands the list of those touched in faith. The movement from Adam and Eve through the Israelites as the chosen people to the extension of the story of salvation attests to the scriptures' extensibility. Beyond the written narrative there is much more to the story. "But there are also many other things which Jesus did; were every one of them to be written, I suppose that the world itself could not contain all the books that would be written" (Jn 21:25).

The scriptural stories are not the only stories to be told. The extensibility and negotiability of the overarching faith story allow for other cultural stories and expressions to be integrated into the narrative. As one reviews the history of evangelization one sees that the cultural narrative may be one of the most important aspects of evangelization. In terms of educational theory, there is the cultural story, juxtaposed with the Christian expression, which then moves through its agent toward a new vision of the Christian story, informed by the culture, which stands on its own.

Each person has within himself or herself a story of the journey through life. It is important that those who are seeking to evangelize look for these stories. The great narratives of history are able to give meaning to these individual stories and add meaning and purpose. The suffering of Christ gives purpose to personal struggles. The stories of the afterlife in major religions give hope to the poor and oppressed. Great romances remind individuals of the beauty of love within the grasp of each of us.

It is also significant that there is an emerging social scientific awareness, which these stories recognize. They may not meet the criteria for empirical evidence, but they withstand the test of time and resonate within the majority of the population. The very sustenance of the great religious stories becomes evidence of their power, truth and learning potential.

Chapter Six

Normative Is Not Typical

While the RCIA process is the normative form of evangelization and entrance into the Church, it is not the typical entrance form for most Christians. Rather, the majority of Christians are baptized, or otherwise Christened, as infants. The entrance progression and their Church *Zones of Proximal Evangelization* (ZPE) begin there and may never end. Much the same way as children come to kindergarten and continue through school, the degree of institutional affiliation will vary according to the individual. In many regards this is as much cultural as it is individual.

The Lifelong Process

The zones of proximal evangelization, the acquisition of language, and the role of story are quite apparent within the RCIA process. The process takes eight months to a year. This specific time parameter is reflective of patterns of learning in other situations, such as early childhood skill development. However, it is the stage development rather than the specific time categories that are most similar to patterns within educational theory. The clearly defined stages, the testimony before the Church, and the ritualized assessments make the RCIA an easy schema to follow for evangelization. Life long evangelization, however, is not as clearly defined.

Life-long learning is a phrase built upon a developmental understanding. Reflecting back upon Shank's (1994) view that "Education is a fundamental human process" (p. 342). Living life is educational. In the same way that educational research often confines education within the parameters of a school setting, evangelization is confined within the Church setting. Both inside and outside of these parameters, there is room for lifelong evangelization.

This creates a semantic difficulty. The RCIA process has clearly defined parameters with which to evaluate a ZPE. Education assesses zones for differing activities at different times. In this section, I will address ZPE for institutional benchmarks, but the scheme for this progression is that one's life is a ZPE. Life long evangelization comes through life long living.

The typical Catholic Christian is baptized into the faith within a few weeks or months of his or her birth. The action is dependent upon the faith of the parent and godparent, since no response is possible from the child. The family raises the child and catechesis takes place according to the family's traditions. Mass attendance, devotional activities, stories of the saints, and celebrations compose the informal setting for the child until he or she is four or five years of age. Each acquisition of a particular skill (making the sign of the cross, learning the Hail Mary, knowing the names of the saints) involves the ZPE.

Once the child comes to church in a more regular or formal manner, classes begin in one form or another. These take various forms and settings: children's liturgy, vacation Bible schools, children's choirs, plays, or children's story time. More regular and structured catechesis begins at age five or six, paralleling the student's secular education.

Formalized education takes place in one or more of three settings: the parochial school, the parish religious education program, or the home. In each setting, a formal curriculum is established for school age children. The first goal of this educational setting is the reception of the Eucharist, which takes place at age seven. The movement from interpersonal faith, dependent upon another, to one's own interiorized faith is seen in the reception of the Eucharist. When the child is able to distinguish bread from the sacramental Christ, he or she is ready to receive the Eucharist.

> For the administration of the Most Holy Eucharist to children, it is required that they have sufficient knowledge and careful preparation so as to understand the mystery of Christ according to their capacity, and can receive the Body

of the Lord with faith and devotion. (Codis Iuris Canonica, 1983, p. 341)

The capacity to receive is more explicitly stated with decisive criteria, "The Most Holy Eucharist may be given to children who are in danger of death, however, if they are able to distinguish the Body of Christ from ordinary food and to receive Communion reverently" (Codis Iuris Canonica, 1983, p. 341). The adult knowledge of the sacrament handed on until automization takes place, when the child distinguishes the sacrament in faith, defines the ZPE.

The catechetical progression of the typical Catholic continues through attendance at Mass, catechetical formation programs, and the home. Neighbors, other Catholics, and the distinct cultural dimensions of certain areas also play an important part in this formation.

The final formal process of the Catholic's ZPE is the reception of confirmation. Here the individual states that he or she believes and is no longer dependent upon the faith of another. "Outside of the danger of death, to be licitly confirmed it is required, if the person has the use of reason, that one be suitably instructed, properly disposed and able to renew one's baptismal promises" (Codis Iuris Canonica, 1983, p. 335).

The typical Catholic's initiation can last as long as sixteen years. While this is dependent upon the diocese and the custom of the region, the majority of US Catholics follow this pattern of initiation. The child begins the journey, a ZPE is established which involves the faith of another, progresses through participation with others through catechesis and participation and ends with the articulation of one's own faith. The truest testimony to completing one's zone of proximal evangelization is the ability to stand-alone and then to invite others into the process themselves. At this point, the initiate becomes the advanced partner or sponsor.

I started this section claiming that there is a lifelong ZPE. The Catholic who follows a typical process of full communion into the Church is not really in the same category as the RCIA entrant. The RCIA presupposes that the process is evangelical. It begins with intention and ends with Baptism and full communion, or entrance into the Church. These two criteria are evidence of evangelization. The typical Catholic, however, fulfills these two criteria before catechesis takes place. In baptism, he or she becomes a member of the Church. Therefore, the ZPE of catechesis takes place, but the semantic problem of evangelization exists. The typical Catholic undergoes evangelization when the goals of evangelization are already achieved, externally. The key to the distinction lies in the Vygotskian formula: " *Stage 3: Where performance is developed, automized, and fossilized. Stage 4: Where deautomization of performance leads to recursion through the zones of proximal development"* [italics theirs] (Gallimore and Tharp, as cited in Moll, pp. 184-185).

The evangelization of one already baptized consists in the development, automization, fossilization, and recursion that are part of the affective sentiments and cognitive understandings associated with belief. The processes of language acquisition and story continue to affect the evangelized throughout life through relationships with others and with cultural elements.

Does the more advanced partner also learn?

The scriptures, the RCIA, Vygotsky, and traditional teacher-centered education all look at the evangelization process from the point of view of the advancement of the lesser learner. Nevertheless, in every relationship of evangelization and education, both partners gain some experience. Cole (1985), and Bruner (1996), Forman and Cazden (1985) all acknowledge the reciprocal nature of learning in some form. In fact, Bruner (1996) defines intersubjectivity as "how humans come to know each other's minds" (p. 12).

Throughout the RCIA process and the typical Catholic's experience there are moments of growth (evangelical and educational) for all involved. The celebration of Baptism gathers members of the family and friends. The infant cannot understand the reading of the Gospel, the pouring of water, the anointing with oil, or the words of the rite. These symbols are for the more advanced learners. Although the object of the action is the child, the words and symbols are efficacious for all present. The Rite of baptism begins with questions to the parents and the godparents, the more advanced learners who address their faith.

The dynamics within the RCIA process set up a dyad between the sponsor or godparent and the new initiate. Within this dyad, the questioning process occurs, both formally and less formally. Both members learn more from going through the process. The godparent or sponsor finds answers that he or she may not know. There are two ways of examining these phenomena. The ZPE is mutual; that is, both learners are learning from their interaction, or each learner has a ZPE that is interacting with another agent.

As an example, the First Communicant receives a scapular for the first time. Not knowing what it is, the child asks the sponsor. Together they determine that it is a devotional item that one wears. The coordinator then explains to the group the meaning of the symbol, earlier unknown to both initiate and sponsor. In this example, the coordinator's explanation solves the problem of this item of devotion for both candidate and sponsor. The first two and the coordinator establish a ZPE. However, there was a mutual coordination of education, knowledge that the scapular is a devotional item one wears, before the most advanced learner entered.

The use of Vygotskian ideas to approach an area of mutual learning is not novel. Many Vygotsky scholars have addressed his work as involving other than a one-way dyadic relationship. Scribner (1985) notes the parallels with adults in other cultural settings, Brown and Ferrara (1985) address the ZPD with disabled children, and Cole (1985) addresses the role of culture.

In addition to the dyadic development possibilities indicated for the sponsor and individual, possibilities also exist between these two and the community, as seen throughout the rites in both the RCIA and the typical progression. The community, acting as a body, calls for a response from the candidate-sponsor team. In the rite, the symbolic placement of the sponsor's hand on the shoulder of the candidate during confirmation bonds the two as they stand in front of the congregation.

The cultural elements and symbols help to establish zones with the individual, candidate-sponsor team, and the community. As one listens to a piece of music, one may go to another for an explanation of the music. However, the music itself, with its lyrics and melody, may draw the learner to a new thinking pattern. A new perception has been advanced because of the introduction of this music. One could say that the music was the catalyst of this thought, or that the group who created the music becomes a "distant" advanced learner, or that the music itself moves the individual and takes the place of the advanced learner.

A reader may believe that one must be sentient to be an advanced learner. In a sense that is true, but since every symbol, work of music, piece of art, or work of architecture has an author or creator, the relationship that is gained through the work is essentially communication with the author. Rather, the beauty and appreciation of created reality is, in fact, an expression of the relationship with God, who is the ultimate advanced learner.

These words, actions, symbols, the things that Christians do, add up to a culture (Bruner 1985, 1997). The culture of Catholicism influences the learning and becomes the more advanced learner for the members of the community. This continued learning or transformational process is part of the continued evangelization of a church member.

This notion that individual ZPE and planes of understanding are transforming each other is alluded to in the work of social psychologists. Vygotsky's concerned himself with planes of interconnectivity, the scaffolding of different levels of thought and possibly even spontaneously created ZPD. And while most psychologists will limit this discussion to the lifelong journey, in light of the goal of evangelization, these planes of learning may even project through the time space continuum of life and death. For now, I will concern myself with physical life.

The label that applies to the learning of all involved in the evangelization process may be debatable. There is strong agreement from educational theorists, however, that some developmental plane or zone exists between the candidate and sponsor and among the candidates, sponsors, community, and cultural symbols. These connections are evident in both the normative and typical forms of evangelization and in the ongoing formative evangelization of believers. There is, therefore, lifelong evangelization in much the same way as there is lifelong learning.

There is the belief, both in evangelization and education, that there is no end to the process. One continues to be educated and to educate, to be converted and to convert. Even after reviewing the normative and typical processes with their easy applications, questions remain. Are there further zones to be achieved at all levels or is there a final level of attainment? Is there directionality? Can someone be lead to a lower level of learning or conversion? In other terms, can there be "diseducation" or negative education? Can the evangelical process be blocked along the way? Is there another sort of multidirectionality in which both the more advanced and the less advanced learners are both learning and changing?

These questions are typical of educational literature, as they are for Church sources. For both fields of inquiry a major question arises: is the normative form of education [interchange "evangelization" here] actually typical? Are schools or churches, while normative, the places where learning takes place most typically?

The interim answer for me is a definite "perhaps, sometimes." Other ways in which the culture can influence this educational and evangelical process will be investigated.

Chapter Seven

Evangelization and Culture

Evangelization affects culture. It is part of the mission of spreading the Gospel to affect the culture in which people relate to one another and God. "The ultimate purpose of mission is none other than to make men share in the communion between the Father and the Son in the Spirit of love[342]" [numbers theirs] (ICCCC, 1995).The Catechism acknowledges another type of barrier to transmission of the faith: "On her pilgrimage, the Church has also experienced the discrepancy existing between the message she proclaims and the human weakness of those to whom the Gospel has been entrusted" (ICCCC, 1995, p. 226). The Church, and her evangelical activity, is asked, not only to establish individual "conversions" but also to establish a culture transformed by the Gospel.

> Missionary endeavor requires *patience*. It begins with the proclamation of the Gospel to peoples and groups who do not yet believe in Christ,[352] continues with the establishment of Christian communities that are 'a sign of God's presence in the world,'[353] and leads to the foundation of local churches. [354] It

must involve a process of inculturation if the Gospel is to take flesh in each
people's culture[355] (ICCCC, 1995, p. 226).

What do the historical Church documents mentioned in previous sections documents say about evangelization? By definition, that it includes the proclamation of Christ, the sharing of the Gospel, the bestowing of baptism upon the unbaptized and the establishment of the Church.

The documents speak of the need for the proclamation of Christ Jesus for faith in order to enjoy salvation, and for entrance into the Church through Baptism. There are three "outs," as it were, to be examined: those, "who through no fault of their own do not know Christ;" those who have received the message via deficient messengers; and the lack of cultural acceptance of the Gospel.

These three areas of examination are not mutually exclusive. The cultural context, the method and effectiveness of delivery, and the formation of the messengers must all be examined in light of each other. The deficiency of messengers may be caused, in part, by the lack of cultural transformation by the Gospel. A recent example would be the number of priests, religious and dedicated laypersons who actively engaged in the massacres between the Hutu and Tutsi tribes. Both tribes are predominantly Catholic and yet rife with division. The culture of these people has not been sufficiently transformed by the Gospel to overcome ancient rivalries and hatreds. In this example, both the messengers and the culture are deficient.

The plethora of monetary improprieties and sexual scandals among clergy in the United States affect their image and morale. Violations of public commitments and trust threaten the credibility of the ordained ministry. The culture of greed, sensuality, and excess offers little support to those living out such public commitments.

Less colorful, but more pervasive, are the messengers who are simply too lazy to do the work necessary to evangelize. Priests, religious and laity have often times found secure niches where minimal activity is required to perform their tasks. Unable to be dislodged from these positions, they become defective messengers by their sheer minimalism of action and purpose.

Related to the lazy are the disinterested. There are many messengers who view evangelization as a word to be discussed, but have little interest in active pursuit of it. Some, claiming that it would be intrusive or anti-ecumenical, prefer to sit back and watch. Those who come to the church doors will receive the standard service, but the disinterested find little reason to "reach out and touch anyone." It is of small import to ask whether those who do not know Christ have been blocked because of individual scandals or because of a culture that has not been transformed by Gospel values.

Church documents articulate a need for individuals to come to Christ. Just as importantly, given the footnotes of "Ad Gentes," is the universal need for promoting the signs of God's presence in the world. As such, the Church is the best possible sign of God's presence; however, as illustrated above, there are times when this transforming presence may be blocked.

Evangelization is Affected by Culture

In his chapter on "Consumer Christianity", Thomas Reeves remarked, "A whopping 84 percent [of those surveyed by Gallup in 1984] said that Jesus was the Son of God, about three-quarters have at some time or another sensed Jesus' presence in their lives, and 66 percent reported having made a personal commitment to Jesus Christ" (Reeves, 1998, p. 51). Reeves also reviewed the figures on Church attendance from several sources, all of which reported them as expressing a high percentage of church attendance or participation. "A 1994 USA Today/CNN/Gallup poll found that 70 percent belonged to a church or synagogue and that 66 percent attended services at least once a month" (Reeves, 1998, p. 53).

Reeves questioned these numbers on the anecdotal evidence that the churches are not full enough to validate these numbers (p. 62). Reeves wonders whether the need to respond that one has attended or regularly attends church may not be, in itself, a reflection of a certain cultural perception of religiosity. Questions of frequency of attendance and the constitution of membership could also be addressed on these grounds.

Although fulfilling one part of the formula of Paul VI by being baptized, some Christians may not accept the teachings of the Church or the manifestations of the Gospel. "America is not—not yet anyway—a thoroughly secular society. But its Christianity, in large part, has been watered down and is at ease with basic secular premises about personal conduct and the meaning of life" (Reeves, 1998, p. 67) . "Religious individualism..." Reeves reminded us, "...is at the core of American Christianity" (p. 62) . Appearing at the same time as the self -report on church attendance poll, another 1988 Gallup poll reported "44 percent of Americans were unchurched (people who said they were not members of any church or had not attended services in the previous six months other than for special religious holidays, weddings, funerals, or the like)"(As cited in Reeves, 1998, p. 61).

In the midst of this conflicting information on actual church attendance, other figures stand out. Figures on crime, domestic violence, poverty, hunger, illiteracy, materialism, and media violence reflect the pervasive nature of these activities. Unless these aspects of society are limited to those individuals who are not attending church or who are not Christians, there is a gap between Baptism, Church attendance and the reality of the Good News.

Evangelization is Fundamentally a Human Process

In an address to the Catholic Educators of the Diocese of Pittsburgh, James Heft, S. M., related that there are the times of grace that are given to us in the sacraments such as the Eucharistic celebration. But there are also the times of grace in the regular activity of our lives (Heft, 1998). These moments of grace may take place within the confines of Church or outside of it. The regular activities of gardening, shopping, nurturing, playing, or sharing a meal may be graceful moments. These moments may occur regularly, as in a family reunion, or singularly, as in a moment when a peculiar smell brings an awareness of God's presence.

These grace-filled moments and activities are not limited to or excluded from church-related activities. One may find a baseball game or work a time of great spiritual awakening and transformation. One may even be so bold as to state that the educational process within the public school system provides moments of grace and touches upon evangelization. Evangelization is not only inherently educational, but education is inherently evangelical.

Evangelization, according to the definition I use, is to make manifest God's loving presence, whose fullness is found in the message and person of Christ, the normative symbol of which is baptism into a community of believers. It also must in part heal the discrepancies caused by deficient messengers, and it must transform cultures. To do this, some very ancient and very new forms of witness and community building must take place.

Yet, even this definition is subject to the discussions presented in this section. God's loving presence, which is made manifest in Christ, may not be presented as Christ explicitly. Rather, through profound and true loving interactions presented to human beings, the message of the Gospel comes alive. These fundamental actions in which God's love is made manifest is fundamental to the human process. To quote St. Iraneus, "the glory of God is man fully alive."

Chapter Eight

Evangelization in Less Typical Forms

At the beginning of this work, I cautioned the reader that my pathway was circuitous. A review of where, it is hoped, I have led the reader at this point follows. Evangelization usually means that one gains entrance into the Church through baptism and membership. The normative form of this is through the RCIA process, but the more typical experience is lifelong evangelization through a series of relationships and experiences. In each of these settings, the categories of learning theory apply. Zones of Proximal Development (or evangelization) are apparent in the evangelization process. Language acquisition and story telling play an important role in the evangelization process. Mediated symbols help to establish further depth in the evangelization and learning processes.

However, outside of the Church experience are millions of people who are either not evangelized or who are not responding to the stories, language, and symbols of the church. It is the task of evangelization to reach out to these people. Using the educational theories already discussed, it would seem that an analysis of their zones, their language, and their stories would help establish a pattern for evangelical progress.

There is another reminder to the reader that is necessary. That is, that evangelization is not always the direct action leading toward entrance into the church. In a broader sense, it is the fostering of better relationship with God. It is moving the individual to a more advanced place in the evangelical continuum. Thus, the non-Christian may become Christian, the veteran Christian becomes more devote, or the sincere seeker simply becomes better (more knowledgeable, more sincere, more understanding, and so on).

The former Minister General of the Order of Friars Minor contextualized this assumption:

> We cannot reduce everything to a single framework. Some distinctions are therefore opportune, indeed often necessary. We realize that it is one thing to evangelize where Christ and his Gospel are totally unknown and another to evangelize where there are already solidly structured and fervent communities, living good Christian lives. It is yet another to work among groups of baptized Christians who are in the process of losing their sense of faith and of belonging to the Church—for whom, in fact, Christ and the Gospel are remote and unreal. (Shalück, 1996, p. 33)

For example, if a person shows a great love and propensity for music, then using music is the appropriate language for evangelization. If that music has a tendency to involve desperate and depraved lyrics, the more advanced learner may attempt to introduce music that is stylistically similar while replacing the lyrics with more hopeful ones. It is not a new idea; it is simply new language and new recognition within our time.

Given all of this, I will present some "secular" experiences that lead people to God or to a higher purpose in life. By recognizing within these experiences the educational partnerships of learner advancement, story, and language, we can also apply the evangelical categories of advancement toward a higher plane.

The twelve-step program of Alcoholic's Anonymous (AA) is possibly the most famous and easiest secular program to compare to the evangelization process. The twelve steps (appendix A) program leads the newcomer into a relationship with the program and the group. Within the process, a sponsor is assigned. The new member moves from initial inquiry in the program to a desire to join. He or she then moves through the steps of the program with the community and sponsor, in much the same way as the RCIA. Anniversaries of sobriety are celebrated and small tokens given to anniversarians.

The partnership of the advanced learner and lesser learner is described in the following terms by AA, "The relative success of the

A. A. program seems to be due to the fact that an alcoholic who no longer drinks has an exceptional faculty for 'reaching' and helping an uncontrolled drinker" (Alcoholics Anonymous [on-line], p.1). The recovered drinker in this pair is considered the more advanced partner.

The evangelical nature of this program is readily apparent. The sober alcoholic chooses a higher power, becomes part of a community, accepts a sponsor, and moves through a process of self-improvement. The process offers a time of grace within human relationship that fits neatly into the definitions given by Tracey and Heft.

The AA program is not much of a leap of faith for most Christians. The process names a higher being or God, it acknowledges prayer and meditation, repentance and retribution. It self-acknowledges a spiritual element. It even has its own evangelical dimension, " Having had a spiritual awakening as the result of these steps, we tried to carry this message to alcoholics and to practice these principles in all our affairs" (Alcoholics Anonymous, [on-line]) .

The AA program makes use of a community approach in which other, more advanced members, those who have been sober longer, support and encourage each other. The encouragement helps to pull the new member through the trials of sobriety and his or her re-establishment of relationships and connections as he or she works through the twelve steps.

The evangelizer can use this program in establishing a base. By understanding the AA process, the evangelizer can recognize the elements of Christian spirituality within it. The assessment of where the individual is and where the individual potential lies can then be determined. An example will help to clarify this.

At first, the program may overwhelm a new member of Alcoholics Anonymous. For the first time in years, he or she is sober. Life is qualitatively better. Relationships are healed and restored, financial stability is regained, and a new self-respect is established. The alcoholic credits all of this to AA. At this point, the AA program becomes for him or her, the Church. The individual's development is a movement toward God.

Language acquisition takes place. The terminology of the twelve steps and slogans such as, '"one day at a time," help to define the experience of the newly sober alcoholic. Story telling, the shared experience of the movement from alcohol to sobriety, becomes part of the regular communal experience.

By evaluating where the individual is on the journey, the evangelizer can then establish the best means of moving the person forward. Bringing a drunken man to his first AA meeting may be the first move in evangelization. Assessing whether she or he is ready to talk to a recovered alcoholic, or move from the AA program to church because of the articulation of a need for a deeper spirituality, may be the next step. In each of these ways, the evangelizer can make use of the language of the individual and his or her ZPD, that is, where the individual is without assistance and where the same individual could be with the assistance of an advanced learner.

The Alcoholics Anonymous program is so familiar to most readers that the spiritual dimensions of the program are easily accepted. To many, it is so similar to a church that the differences are negligible. However, what about even less religious forms where the concept of God or a higher being are not articulated?

Art

Great works of art have always been used to communicate the divine. The image that most perfectly summarizes the work of this study graces the ceiling of the Sistine Chapel. There, Michelangelo, in the great tradition of educational theorists, depicts Adam and his most basic ZPE. Limp and without life, the zone of what man is versus what he can be with God (the advanced learner) is depicted in full color. While neither Michelangelo nor Vygotsky thought of each other in their work, they both express the idea of a "time-space moment" where each individual can be reach the highest potential. This space or zone can be identified throughout the evangelization process as humanization and divinization come together. Art helps to bring new insight into the dignity and mystery of the human experience.

Religious art inspires and instructs. The story of the older Guatemalan man asking questions about the artistic representation of Christ or the Italian woman understanding ecclesiology through the representation of Mary are easily identified. But can art evangelize? Does it bring one to a new awareness or heightened state? The simple answer is yes.

> Conversion has been described as ravishing our senses by the grace of God. God's love radiates through the whole person, setting all afire—senses, intellect, emotions, will. For example, a person may become aware of Jesus' saving love for the first time while gazing at a crucifix. The total person becomes deeply affected by this graced scene, to the point of prolonged change of heart and behavior. (Polutanovich, 1991, p.91) .

However, just as with Alcoholics Anonymous program or Church membership it depends upon the original situation of the person and the potential for development.

Vygotsky originally used the ZPD as an alternative to IQ testing to examine potential. A different translation of ZPD may help to clarify the use of the concept. Many European and Latin American translations use the term "Social Area of Potential Development." While this does not change the basic concept or its application, it does give the reader a sense of its broader application. The zone includes the cultural history of each subject. This terminology may help the reader to look at evangelization through social constructivist development.

Using the educational concepts of potential developmental zones, can we declare that art helps to bring people to a greater understanding or heightened belief? The objection may also arise that constructivist or co-constructivist understandings can only happen between individuals.

In classrooms throughout the world, teachers engineer environments for management and learning. While the teacher is the ultimate source of this engineered environment, the immediate interaction is between the learner and the environment. In the same way, the use and management of art can help to engineer development. It is not the teacher-child relationship, but the child-environment relationship that is part of the educational process.

In visual art, there are the possibilities of the object of art acting as a catalyst (or stimulus, if this term does not cause too much confusion) for an individual. A person who arranges the art may serve as an advanced learner. Still another person may help the original individual to find meaning in the art. To complicate matter, each of these "persons" may be groups of people or may have cumulative effect upon meaning for the original viewer. "Developing culturally, a child gains the opportunity to *create himself those stimuli that in the future will influence him, organize his behavior,* and attract his attention"(Vygostky & Luria, 1993, p. 189 [italics theirs]) .

The multifaceted aspects of the art-learner pairing are complicated. However, Moll & Greensburg (1990) addressed this as part of the natural learning process. It involves diffuse forms and multiple persons. Yet, the placement of art can begin instruction, evangelization, and greater self-understanding within a cultural context. Take for example this section of a story by Susan Sontag (1987),

> And Xavier brought an eighteenth-century Guatemalan
> wooden statue of St [sic.] Sebastian with upcast eyes and
> open mouth, and when Tanya said what's that, a tribute to

eros past, Xavier said where I come from Sebastian is
venerated as a protector against pestilence. Pestilence
symbolized by arrows? Symbolized by arrows. All people
remember is the body of a beautiful youth bound to a tree,
pierced by arrows (of which he always seems oblivious,
Tanya interjected), people forget that the story continues,
Xavier continued, that when the Christian women came to
bury the martyr they found him still alive and nursed him
back to health. And he said, according to Stephen, I didn't
know St Sebastian didn't die. It's undeniable, isn't it, said
Kate on the phone to Stephen, the fascination with dying.
(p. 29)

Although a story, a piece of art is presented. It speaks to the viewer
with an immediate story dependent upon culture. At once the statue is a
tortured youth, a martyred saint, and a resuscitated confessor. The art
piece remains the same, yet the relationship takes place with the statue,
the story, others and the original artist and saint. Each can be dissected
and analyzed for lesser and advanced learners. Theologically, this can
be expressed as,

An icon or a cross does not simply exist to direct our
imagination during our prayers. It is a material center in
which there reposes an energy. A divine force, which unites
itself to human art. (Lossky as cited in Polutanovich, 1991,
p.90) .

Each element can be described in social proximal development. And
the entire whole can be viewed as moving the people involved into
greater understandings and a heightened belief in life. Through this one
piece, evangelization takes place.

Photography

Photography is a relatively modern expression of art in the history
of humanity. When one thinks of art, one may think in terms of
sculpture, painting, or the more ancient forms. Often photography does
not garner the same level of respect, as do the more classical forms.
Part of this image comes from the perception that a photographer does
not add artistry into his or her work, but simply captures what is
already present. However, there are certain images, captured in time
and space that change individuals and whole societies.

Any reader who lived through the days of the Vietnam War will
remember the cover of *Life* magazine where a young girl was depicted

running away from a napalm attack. A younger reader may recall the images of war, of poverty, of crime, as well as images of beauty. Sontag puts the view of the photographer in perspective:

> The photographer was thought to be an acute but non-interfering observer—a scribe, not a pot. But people quickly discovered that nobody takes the same picture of the same thing, the supposition that cameras furnish an impersonal, objective image yielded to the fact that photographs are evidence not only of what's there but of what an individual sees, not just a record but an evaluation of the world. (Sontag, 1977, p. 88)

The photographic image, once again, leads an individual into a unique relationship with the subject of the photograph or the photographer. The influence of multi-dimensional photography such as movies and television add, not only the power of the image, but also the relationships of sight and sound and story. The power of each aspect of artistry can come alive in each dimension or in the cumulative whole.

Literature

The role of literature is similarly to inspire, educate and bring awe. It is not only the scriptural stories, but also the stories of life in general. Sontag relates:

> Well, it does educate us about life. I wouldn't be the person I am, I wouldn't understand what I understand, were it not for certain books. I'm thinking of the great question of nineteenth-century Russian literature: how should one live? A novel worth reading is an education of the heart. It enlarges your sense of human possibility, of what human nature is, of what happens in the world. It's a creator of inwardness. (Sontag, 1995, p. 193)

The reader will, it is hoped, perceive the similarities in the evangelization process and in constructivist educational theory. The move toward "inwardness" is expressed in social psychological terms as intrapersonal. The reading and story bring people to a new level of understanding through animation unique to their receptivity. This is, of course, historically and culturally mediated.

Once again, there is the need to address whether the object (art) necessarily evokes a relationship. The piece of art or literature that goes unnoticed or unperceived is of little consequence or of similar consequence to the great mass of people with whom we do not choose to relate. In each case, this may be a sad commentary on life, but it is not the focus of this study. Rather, when perceived or examined, is there a relational aspect with the work of art?

The response to this has already been examined in relation to the social cultural psychologists' responses. But there is a correlation in the artistic dimension by Sontag:

> For defenders of the real from Plato to Feurbach to equate image with mere appearance—that is, to presume that the image is absolutely distinct from the object depicted—is part of the process of desacralization which separates us irrevocably from the world of sacred times and places in which an image was taken to participate in the object depicted. (Sontag, 1973, p. 155)

Thus, in the sacralization or evangelization, an equity of terms that I hope the reader allows, the image can and must bring us into relationship with itself or its author and move us forward in human and divine progress. Concisely, the experience with the image moves us, changes us, and educates us.

The vocabulary and imagery of church no longer is the exclusive, if even the primary venue for finding the transcendental. Therefore, how do we identify that which can be the *locus theologicus* for our time and place? We find it in the individual's language and social development. We must reintegrate into church and secular life the experiences that continue to move people.

Lighted candles have never lost meaning. The warmth and glow of a flame have the enduring intimacy that every generation has come to experience. The freshness of water and the imagery that is so strong and sensual that it can never escape any human— chains, a swazsticher, fire, bread, blood, black, and red— these are the intimate, religious, human/divine images which cross cultures and touch hearts. What are the signs and symbols within the psyche of the postmodern understanding that can express the deeper truth of the divine?

As we enter the twenty-first century with a new power of word and image, we also enter with a new concept of truth. The way that we bring the message of the Gospel to people is inextricably connected to their symbols, their modes of communication, the experiences of receiving and editing and censoring data and imagery, and the power of expression that is now available to us.

> Since Christianity is an incarnational religion, it reflects the
> goodness of matter and object: the Word was made flesh
> and dwells among us. We go to God through images and
> not just ideas. Christ redeemed humankind so that mind,
> will, imagination, senses emotions, matter—the total
> person and all creation— are raised in Christ.
> (Polutanovich, 1991, p. 90).

Christians used the sensuality of the Baptismal ritual, artists used the
colors of glass to teach the illiterate, the monks illumined scrolls to
interpret texts and entertain while passing on the sacred message.
Today, the ability to design new images and virtual reality brings even
more challenges to the worlds of education and evangelization.

> The emergence of a visual or image culture and the
> concomitant development of virtual reality technologies
> pose a challenge, in general, to a culture which has been
> largely transmitted by written word, and, in particular, to
> cultural traditions such as religious life which considers
> literary texts among the definitive, normative expressions
> of community identity. (Johnson, 1995, p. 24)

The myriad ways of bringing new meaning to people is growing
exponentially. Educational theorist attempt to keep pace with
movements of technology and information. These rapid developments
impact all areas in which word and symbol are involved. Traditional
approaches in both education and evangelization relied upon a cohesive
family unit. This unit changed drastically during the industrial era and
even more intensely in this age of information. The delivery of the
"meaning message" will also change in its shape and form.

This new delivery of the message comes in a difficult culture. The
United States was, as every school child knows, a melting pot. This is a
metaphor rejected by many today because it does an injustice to the
individual cultural expressions that come together in the United States.
It may also do damage to the experience of art and symbol that I am
addressing. Camille Paglia (1994) opines,

> In our culture, under the influence of Protestantism, there
> has been this homogenization, this constant bleaching out
> of everything ethnic in America. As that happens we get
> more and more removed from the life of the body. Even
> though the body is tortured in Catholic iconography, it's
> still there, it's present. But in Protestantism, in Presbyterian
> and Episcopalian styles, which is very chi-chi (where I

grew up the businessmen were always Presbyterian), it's a very bland, country-club style. (p. 3)

The commentary is not an attack on Protestantism. It is the pain felt from loss of imagery. Since the Second Vatican Council the Church has simplified and removed many images. The sentient experience of Church has changed. "There's nothing gloomy, nothing majestic, nothing awesome. And even the candles are gone! The elemental flame when you would light a candle" (Paglia, 1994, p. 3) .

Paglia's descriptions speak of the evocative and relational element within images. In order to reach the ultimate depths of human existence and transform them, images must be presented that can draw people into relationship and reflect their spiritual and emotional needs. The selection of these images, the ways of presenting images, and the relationships they engender will be dependent upon the individuals involved. Just as there is no piece of art that receives unanimous acclamation for its perfection, there is no one way to evangelize people. We must offer more depth, color, passion, and skill so as to advance the entire race.

Of course, the beauty and artistry of the stark Puritan, Mennonite, and other minimalist traditions also bring opportunities for advancement. "Artistic expression provides a tool for evangelization, bringing people in deeper contact with God and their own humanness" (Polutanovich, 1991, p.90) .

Relationship

Ultimately, evangelization's concern is with one's relationship with God and other. As is reflected throughout my paper there is "...the tension between a purely Christian evangelization aimed at enhancing the influence of Christian religion in the larger culture, and an evangelization linked to a sense of the church's social ministry and aimed at transforming an entire culture and, ultimately, in forwarding the Kingdom of God" (O'Brien, 1993, p.47) . The transforming qualities of life are evident in so many ways, as art, music, architecture, and all the sentient experiences. In each moment, there is a teachable and preachable moment.

In each person's history there are true person-to-person connections that help to transform him or her. Sometimes this transformation takes place as a result of one of the aforementioned sentient experiences. The Guatemalan man is led to as a priest for an explanation, the Italian woman teaches the novice, the social activists bind together for support. Often the transformational experience is developed from an attraction or infatuation and may move toward love.

Then, there are the special moments that, I hope, occur in almost every person's life and are not peculiar to me: the moments when human solidarity and God's presence make themselves known in a unique way. These are the moments, in a smoke filled bar, when one sits back and looks at humanity attempting to interact, to relate, to be more human. There are times when a cause stirs people to become one body to address some wrongdoing or some great joy. In schools, this is often seen when a winning sports team goes on to the finals. An indescribable solidarity takes place as a result of such simple catalysts. They are the moments when people "belong," when they feel that there is something more than their corporate selves are working together as a whole. There may not be great goals, ("I just want to talk to this woman"), but, there are regular moments when people get together that God is present. There is very little difference between Shank's, "... Any time you put three people together, within a few minutes one person will be teaching something to the other two" (Shank, 1994, p. 342) and the Gospel's "Wherever two or three of you are gathered in my name." The human action of gathering and relating is both natural and supernatural. It leads towards greater understanding.

Chapter Nine

De-Evangelization or Diseducation

What about the role of the negative? Are there ways in which art, music, literature, gatherings, can be evil? Can two or three people come together in God's name and God be present, but as a saddened participant? When people naturally teach one another, is it possible that the teaching will lead into ignorance rather than enlightenment?

The Ku Klux Klan (KKK), to be sure, as they gather together, makes use of every element that I have addressed. They gather in darkness and gloom (Paglia, 1994), they costume themselves to add focus and mystery (Polutanovich, 1991), they make use of the Internet for their message (Johnson, 1995), and they gather together in education (Shank, 1994) and in evangelization—at least, in their form. But is this educative or holy?

I have used this example because it is the most frightening to me. A group that gathers for reasons of hatred and ignorance according to my personal standards make use of the very name and symbols that I hold the most sacred. My heart and soul tell me that this group and others are anti-education and anti-evangelization.

That, however, is not a logical conclusion. Education is not only educative when it successfully teaches those things which are believed to be good by the majority or even by a minority. To educate about the working of nuclear weapons is probably believed to be a good by the United States military, even when the use of nuclear weapons would be an horrific evil. Is the newcomer being diseducated?

A Christian who chooses to become Muslim or Jewish or Wiccan is entering into a form of recruitment or evangelization (to use the Christian term). While some Christians may see this shift of allegiance as a move toward a lesser form of worship or even away from salvation, is this disevangelization? What if this movement away brings someone to a more meaningful view of humanity and divinity and behaviors that are more loving? In this case, the "de-evangelization" may be evangelizing.

There is no reason to believe that every symbol, group, experience, or sound will be good and holy or that all symbols are of equal value. Obviously, there are those works of literature, art, music, gardening, architecture, and philosophy that have withstood the test of time. To believe in a radical equality of symbol would be to embrace indifferentism. Rather, I return to Kung (1988), that there is a difference between the religious and the psuedoreligious.

The radical equality is present in the personal search, the difference between objective religion and subjective religion. This is a distinction that Americans have difficulty in accepting. If an experience is good for me, then the structure should change to accept it for everyone. This is not always true. Divorce is seen as a failure of a commitment. Yet, for many men and women the break of a bond in divorce was a subjectively positive experience as compared to the suffering that took place in the days, months, and years of a dead relationship. This does not have as a resulting meaning that divorce is good, but that it has some subject value for the individuals in spite of its objective negative value.

No institution, organization, relationship, or symbol can reflect every person's reality. To do such would be to destroy the uniqueness of each of these. Because a Matisse brings joy to one person, it doesn't mean that everyone will or should take joy in viewing a Matisse. Similarly, if one finds great hope in the writings of Ghandi, it doesn't follow that all must become non-violent. Paglia (1994) points out the historical revisionist tendencies and current a current example.

> That's the problem even with the gay argument. I've taken the position all along that "the Bible condemns homosexuality." It does, O.K. ? I just hate this going back to history and saying, "Well, it makes people feel bad now that people thought that then," and trying to re-write it by claiming, "Oh no, the story of Sodom is not about

homosexuality, it was really about hospitality. " I hate these sentimental fantasies.

But the public realm: Let's take for example of pornographic magazines. I maintain that pornographic magazines must be available universally. A Christian person coming out of the subway should not have to be assailed at the newsstand by a row of naked ladies on the fronts of magazines. (p. 4)

So, in symbol and experience, the evangelizer, and the advanced learner must assess the personal use of symbol and the impact of these symbols on the individual. There is not an acceptance of the symbol, music, or system as objectively better, but an acceptance that there may be a subjective value in the journey of the individual or community expressed through each of these. The sharing of the awareness may also bring to the partner new insight into the beauty and understanding of the language being used.

The distinctions become less clear. Let me add more ambiguity. If we believe that there are "good ends" and "bad ends" to both evangelization and education, are there also "good means" and "bad means" ? For centuries the Catholic Church restricted the books that adherents could read because of the harm they might do. In art, most people believe that there are certain images that are good and holy, or at least proper and respectable. "In the Western church there was a specific artistic stance. The object could be pleasing aesthetically and teach a religious dogma" (Polutanovich,1991, p. 91). However, there is also the view that every image can bring about a new awareness of beauty and love. "There are Hindu temples where you have nothing but huge facades with intertwined couples. And threesomes! And foursomes! And that's considered sacred—in tantric yoga. Copulating bodies, exposure of genitals, that is a form of spiritual exhibitionism that is considered an honoring of the fertility principle" (Paglia, 94, p. 5). Are there only certain "good" means by which evangelization may move forward? If a piece of art that is objectively vulgar or even worthless in terms of its artistry brings one to a revelation about life and his or her place in the divine plan, then is this piece of art to be deleted from the images that may be rightly used to evangelize? Any and every piece of art, music, Internet site, creation experience, even if objectively perceived as inappropriate, may be prescriptively evangelical for an individual.

The current running throughout these pages is that similarities exist between education and evangelization. There may be a significant division at this point. Education is fundamental and human (Shank, 1994). In every activity, we are learning. Regardless of the national debate on the quality of education, the reality is that students and adults are learning. The debates that rage truly revolve around whether the results and foci of learning are those that we wish. Our students in educational institutions may be learning about truancy, drug use and violence, but that is still learning. There is no way, with possible exceptions of brain surgery or memory loss, that education is not dynamic and constructive. Even if one learns to play the piano incorrectly and must, to use a common expression, "unlearn" in order to learn the correct form, the individual is not then incapable of performing the action incorrectly if desired. And in cases where memory and time have worn away past learning, it is not that we have withdrawn or receded into an area of ignorance; it is simply that our long-term storage capabilities may not be efficaciously activated. Or, in terms of body memory; one may never forget how to ride a bicycle, but have physical disabilities that in later life preclude him or her from this activity. However, none of these examples involve a "dislearning" or refutation of learning.

One may argue that to lead another into ignorance is a disservice and a form of diseducation. However, even if the more advanced learner, say in the KKK example, leads a person into the midst of KKK lore and practice, it is not that the process of education is missing or faulty; it is the perceived result that is heinous and despicable. Thus, an advanced learner does not have directionality in the sense of being able to avoid all education with another. The advanced learner, however, can impact the result of that education. A less emotion filled example might be in order.

If a young child is paired with another, more advanced partner in an arithmetic class, learning theory may conclude that the lesser learner would be pulled forward by the more advanced learner. If the more advanced learner assists the lesser learner until the lesser learner can perform the arithmetic work given in the same way as the advanced learner, yet both are doing the work incorrectly, it does not mean that learning did not progress forward. Instead, it means that the focus and result of this pairing did not achieve the desired outcome.

This may be the dividing point. Can evangelization be evangelical if it does not raise the person to a new and more loving level of existence? A limitation that I cannot address is the multitude of meanings that "more loving" can take. One could argue that the KKK member believes him or herself to be more loving in his or her perception. I hesitate to base a view on the "normative" position because it will then call into question earlier logical steps in assessing beauty and efficacy in subjective areas. However, I will assume, some will argue falsely or illogically, that the end of evangelization must be some higher, more beautiful, and more loving form. A form that is recognizable to people of good will as such. Creation spirituality may give some focus to this dilemma. "God is perceived as being truly present everywhere and in all things. So they respect other human beings as the temples of God, and they respect the earth and all its creatures as God's dwelling places" (McLaughlin, J., 1993, p. 201). The difference between evangelization and education is that evangelization must have this goal of a more loving end, because God is love.

Practical Matters

Evangelization could not only occur outside of the Church but could also lead someone away from the Church. Practically this may cause concern for Catholics or Christians in general. This is as much a semantic problem as a theological one. Obviously, if God is love and the church is established as God's community of love, then anyone moving forward in love moves forward toward the Church. However, even the specificity of letter case becomes important as we realize that while one may remain faithful, even become more faithful to the church, he or she may leave the Church.

The nominal Catholic who has attended a local parish for decades may find a new relationship with God by worshipping with a Buddhist monastic community. The movement toward Buddhism may objectively seem like a movement away from the Gospel. Subjectively, the experience may enhance the individual's love and power to transform the world into God's Kingdom.

During the decades of the nineteen seventies and eighties Church groups gathered together according to legislation pending on the Capitol Hill. Coalitions that needed to be according to social issues that were in vogue: Central America, hunger, women, etcetera. These people came together from a variety of church/theological backgrounds. In many cases, they very much disagreed with the specific doctrine or politics of their congregations, but they remained very loyal to them. Furthermore, they grouped themselves into social action units in which they worked, prayed, even lived together in a way that truly expressed their "religious" conviction. The issues and the "symbols" of these people are not the creedal formulae, but rather action statements on hunger, oppression, and dignity. In many cases the lobbying groups themselves became alternative ecclesial communities, linked by the advocacy issues that influenced them.

These movements may become more subject to debate as the communities of choice become less benign. Another Christian realizes that he or she is homosexual. The perceived oppression of the Christian community forces the individual to seek support and encouragement in another setting. This setting, such as the Metropolitan Church or a gay activist association becomes a type of church community in much the same way as does the AA, or an art colony, or a musical group. Each of these places or groups allows encouragement and education.

To state that these communities offer support and advancement toward love is not to say that they are not ever to be critiqued. In each community there are deficiencies of expression that keep them from their task of advancement. Camille Paglia, who earlier suggested liberal artistic expression, criticizes ACT UP, the gay activist group, as "nihilistic" and proposes that feminists must respect the pro-life position more (Paglia, 1994) . The criticisms and the constant striving to change and transform an organization are part of the dynamism of God's work in creation.

This brings me to the heart of the question. If there are so many similarities between education and evangelization, and if evangelization and education occur so naturally and in so many venues, why bother to do anything? The answer becomes personal and pragmatic.

While there are many possibilities in the world for seeing the vestiges of God in His creation, there is also the belief that the greatest potential for this vision exists within the Church. Even more specifically, it is my personal belief that the greatest potential is found within the confines of the Catholic Church in communion with Rome. This belief does not injustice to those who believe otherwise and there is no anti-ecumenical spirit in my statement. If I did not believe this, I would not belong to this Church.

Since I hold this belief, I can now look at the similar situation in education. If I wish to structure a situation for particular learning, it does not negate the role of learning outside of that structure; it simply allows me to focus myself upon a purposeful task. Education does take place in schools. By using social constructivist theories, I may be able to assess and apply better learning opportunities to arrive at my desired result. By evaluating certain zones or activating prior knowledge, or using authentic tasks, I may help others to advance to a predetermined goal in a more successful manner.

In evangelization, then, one must know the goal. We know that God works in the world. How do we cooperate in that effort within the structure that has the most potential, while respecting and enhancing the forms of God's work outside of the structure?

Chapter Ten

Conclusions

The world has art, and music, and poetry to show forth the love of God. Education shows us that one program does not fit all. We must utilize the prior knowledge and experience of each evangelical candidate and juxtapose experience that will lift him or her to new levels. The uniqueness of this view is that some images, though secular, even repulsive, may lead a person to new and advanced understanding. Music that would be considered an assault by some, or writing that is believed heretical, may actually and truly lift the individual to a new belief and vision of God.

The Church is uniquely positioned to accept this view of evangelization. As one of the few non-commercial, truly universal organizations, she has the breadth of experience to promote true evangelical dialogue. However, in order to place Christians in positions where they can dialogue with artists, musicians, Internet media specialists, authors, poets, dancers, activists, Buddhists, economists, and the like, they must be educated in these same fields with the understanding that their content area contributes to the evangelical mission of the Church. The "New Evangelization" means that all content areas of human existence have evangelical purpose. This will certainly test the patience of the Congregation for the Doctrine of the Faith.

What is new about this approach? In reality, there is nothing new about the conclusions. We are simply called to return to their unique position of seeing evangelical possibilities in all things. The gate through which this approach is being seen is the educational one. However, there is a new language acquisition that can occur using education. If evangelizers begin to view people in terms of zones of development and individual story and language, then freshness exists in this approach.

The role of evangelization must be more courageous. In the past, "Catholic evangelization, then, was aimed at Catholics themselves, and had as its goal to cement institutional loyalties and strengthen group life" (O'Brien, 1993, p. 52) . The goal of evangelization must be the hope for transforming the world for the Kingdom, rather than just the strengthening the local parish community.

The equivalence of educational theory and theological hermeneutics comes to its logical conclusion. There are advanced and lesser learners in every field and endeavor. The mutuality of learning and teaching is the pattern of relational life that brings meaning to the world. This can be expressed through Vygotsky's ZPD or the stages of the RCIA. The acquisition of language in each field brings with it the ability to express inner realties of life. Just as a child learns to ask for a cookie or a drink, so too does a person of faith learn to articulate the experiences of God in his or her life. It is the task of the evangelizer, just as that of a teacher, to enter these experiences to help develop the faith language and to deepen his or her own faith articulation.

This approach will take great effort. It is means that every cultural symbol must be evaluated in terms of its value in bringing the kingdom to fruition. Instead of assigning items as sacred or perverse, more gray areas must enter the dialogue. The question, "What does this mean for you?" must become part of the common language of evangelization.

Individuality is a primary concern. In the areas of both education and evangelization attempts were made to establish institutional programs that teach and preach the basic messages to all people. These attempts have not achieved their desired results. By assessing, their present position, their aspirations, dreams, hopes, and beliefs through dialogue, he or she may then respond to advance the individual or group toward the goal of further relationship with God. In doing so, the evangelizer also recognizes new footprints of God in the experience of the individual or group and so furthers his or her own development.

The greatest challenge to this form of evangelization is that it is at the same time simple and dynamically complex. To simply live life, experiencing it to the fullest with others and looking for the signs of God and helping others to see these, is much more difficult than simply standing and pointing to a definitive symbol and creed. No longer is priest or religious the sage to whom others come to find truth; rather he is the brother or sister who shares in the struggles and finds meaning in the collective experience of such.

There are major problems with this work. The first is that it has too many theological ambiguities. I am allowing God to do too much work. If Christ has redeemed the world, then all things are good again. This does not leave enough room for evil. Hatred and violence, persecution and torture are not of God. They may be educational, but they oppose God's will.

The opposite theological problem also exists. Does this approach, in which all of creation provides opportunities for grace, presume that humans can work out their own salvation, as long there is a correct orientation toward love? This is the difficulty that was faced by liberation theologians, believing that, if society through communal action could end injustice and oppression, they could build the Kingdom of God. I am not suggesting this.

By applying educational theory to evangelization, we can simply assess where an individual is on his or her journey and apply the methods or objects that might better assist the furtherance of this journey toward God. In a sense, this is prescriptive evangelization. There is the utter reliance upon God, through Christ, to make all things new again and therefore allow us to cooperate through creation and relationship in the salvific process.

I have also attempted to isogete Vygotsky and other educational psychologists into evangelization where they do not naturally fit. Story, language, and symbol are natural expressions of both realms, education and evangelization, but the manner of application and the studies of these applications are not necessarily synonymous. Throughout my writing, I believed that Vygostky and other atheist educational psychologists might roll over in their respective graves if they were to read that their concepts were being applied to evangelization.

Questions still remain. The foremost of these is whether one can tailor signs and images, stories and language to fit a particular agenda for evangelization. Public relations agencies and spin-doctors attempt to tailor information in a way that leads an individual into a particular understanding of a story or interpretation. They have been very successful with this medium within the political sphere. The age of

Christendom attempted to use the signs, symbols, metaphors and stories of Christianity to surround the believer and so influence his or her thoughts and beliefs. Can we still do this, as a church, in the new millennium? Do we want to do this in an age of pluralism? There is the possibility, that we can use effective evangelization to help transform everyone into similarly thinking members of the same church. Or, we can become a universal Kingdom of God by allowing ourselves to be transformed by the experience of God's love in each other. The difference depends on how open we are to the zones of evangelization between ourselves and that Most Advanced Learner–God.

Appendix A

The Twelve Steps of Alcoholics Anonymous

The relative success of the A.A. program seems to be due to the fact that an alcoholic who no longer drinks has an exceptional faculty for "reaching" and helping an uncontrolled drinker.

In simplest form, the A.A. program operates when a recovered alcoholic passes along the story of his or her own problem drinking, describes the sobriety he or she has found in A.A., and invites the newcomer to join the informal Fellowship.

The heart of the suggested program of personal recovery is contained in Twelve Steps describing the experience of the earliest members of the Society:

1. We admitted we were powerless over alcohol - that our lives had become unmanageable.

2. Came to believe that a Power greater than ourselves could restore us to sanity.

3. Made a decision to turn our will and our lives over to the care of God as we understood Him.

4. Made a searching and fearless moral inventory of ourselves.

5. Admitted to God, to ourselves and to another human being the exact nature of our wrongs.

6. Were entirely ready to have God remove all these defects of character.

7. Humbly asked Him to remove our shortcomings.

8. Made a list of all persons we had harmed, and became willing to make amends to them all.

9. Made direct amends to such people wherever possible, except when to do so would injure them or others.

10. Continued to take personal inventory and when we were wrong promptly admitted it.

11. Sought through prayer and meditation to improve our conscious contact with God as we understood Him, *praying only for knowledge of His will for us and the power to carry that out.*

12. Having had a spiritual awakening as the result of these steps, we tried to carry this message to alcoholics and to practice these principles in all our affairs.

Newcomers are not asked to accept or follow these Twelve Steps in their entirety if they feel unwilling or unable to do so.

They will usually be asked to keep an open mind, to attend meetings at which recovered alcoholics describe their personal experiences in achieving sobriety, and to read A.A. literature describing and interpreting the A.A. program.

A.A. members will usually emphasize to newcomers that only problem drinkers themselves, individually, can determine whether or not they are in fact alcoholics.

At the same time, it will be pointed out that all available medical testimony indicates that alcoholism is a progressive illness, that it cannot be cured in the ordinary sense of the term, but that it can be arrested through total abstinence from alcohol in any form.

(Alcoholics Anonymous, 1999)

Appendix B

The Franciscan Program

Differing theological perspectives and philosophical stances have led to particular interpretations throughout history. This appendix is provided to give a brief historical, philosophical and cultural theological context for this work. It is my belief that the Franciscan Order by its nature and history is most suited for new forms of evangelical exploration.

History

How have Franciscans evangelized in the past? Remembering that the Franciscan Order is more than 800 years old, we can say that the answer to this question is dependent upon time, place, definition, and personalities. In each time and place the response has been different, yet there is a similar pattern in each era and culture. These patterns are built upon a philosophical basis, which allows for the goodness of humanity and the diversity of form. Franciscans have made use of every sentient experience possible for evangelization, choosing symbols, songs, smells, even tastes that reflect God in the culture being addressed. In thirteenth century Italy this meant introducing the vernacular for prayer and music. Today's symbols may be distinct, but must be authentic and relevant in the same way that the chosen symbols of evangelization have been throughout the ages.

Possibly the most definitive work on Franciscan evangelization throughout the ages is by Agostino Gemelli, OFM. Writing a chronological summary of Franciscan achievements, published in 1935, Gemelli traces the Order's history and accomplishments century by century until the date of publication. I rely heavily upon this work as the outline for this section.

The story of St. Francis must be the starting point. Assisi, Italy gave birth to the son of a young merchant, who reflected everything the culture of his time held dear. Italian politics, the influx of the vernacular, the troubadour tradition, the rise of a merchant class, religious strife, military conquests, all influenced him (Bonaventure, 1509, trans. 1973; Celano, 1229, trans. 1973; Gemelli, 1935). These cultural influences affected his interpretation of the Gospel and the beginnings of the Order he established.

The Franciscan tradition allows for diversity. Francis blesses Brother Elias, the administrator who will pump up the machinery of the Order, as well as Brother Leo, the humble, prayerful, beggar (Gemelli, 1935, p. 53) . While admonishing the brothers to be content with being unlettered (Francis of Assisi, 1223, trans. 1973, p. 63), St. Francis gives St. Anthony permission to study. Francis forbids money, property, even animals, but accepts the gift of Mount LaVerna and tells the friars never to leave the Portiuncula (Celano, 1229, trans. 1973). This diversity has been a hallmark of the Franciscan program.

The Rule of 1223 strictly forbids the use of money by the friars (Francis of Assisi, 1223, trans. 1973, p. 60). Through this prohibition, Francis binds the brothers, not only to the providence of God, but to work and to reliance upon others. The insistence upon work for the friars, or begging if there was no work, had a two-fold result. It caused equity within the brotherhood between those from higher social strata who never previously had worked and it caused the friars to relate to others. Whether in the bartering of food for work or the call for alms, the brothers were forced into relationship. Even more novel was the fact that they reversed the norm of relationship between religious and lay people. Religious were dependent upon the goodness of the laity as opposed to the lay dependence upon the great monasteries. There was a consecration of the ordinary modes of daily life through the friars' example.

Francis is well known for the establishing of Christmas customs. He began the tradition of the Christmas manger, he established Christmas carols and sang in the vernacular (Bonaventure, 1509, trans. 1973; Celano, 1229, trans. 1973). The telling of local tales in the common language, as opposed to Latin, allowed stories greater influence in the daily lives of common folk. Francis borrowed the troubadour's mode of operation, plus the ancient stories of the local people, and adapted them to tell the Gospel story. Beyond this, from the very beginning he established himself and the brotherhood among people. In doing this, he and the brothers remained culturally in tune with their surroundings.

The pattern of Franciscan evangelization becomes the affirmation of ordinary culture and life. An appreciation for diversity, the use of common symbols, songs, language, and the intimate contact with culture and people will define Franciscan evangelization throughout the centuries.

Philosophical Basis

The history of philosophy in the Franciscan Order can be traced to its roots in Augustinian Platonism. This form of Platonism, a "perversion" according to Harris (1927, p. 236) was not opposed to Aristotle but a sort of syncretism of both with additions. This is important because it gives meaning to the very nature of the Franciscan program.

> Franciscan idealism was grafted naturally on to the main trunk of Augustinian Platonism, because its intuition of the meaning of the universe, its love of beauty, its development of human will-power, its craving to enter into touch with the divine, all postulate solutions similar to those found in the doctrines of St. Augustine. (Gemelli, 1935, p. 55)

Alexander of Hales took this philosophy and formed it into a school of thought. "In his Theodicy he developed the idea of a providential Goodness presiding over all creation, the cult of the Trinity which leaves its impress on all things, and the religious sense of beauty in man leading the soul Godwards" (Gemelli, p. 55). This statement is the very essence of Franciscan evangelization. Beauty, found in all things, leads a person to God. Therefore, even ordinary forms of education and educational theory fit this pattern.

St. Bonaventure developed from this philosophy a precursor to semiotic understanding. "Though he (Bonaventure [emphasis mine]) did not arrive at a formulation of the problem of aesthetic beauty in the modern sense, he established, in a way that no one—not even the Greeks—had ever done before, its psychological elements" (Gemelli, 1935, p. 56) . Bonaventure stressed the subjective relationship between beauty and the individual. He was able to capture the emotional experience of the subject and passed this perspective on to the Franciscan school. By reflecting upon the mysticism of St. Francis,

Bonaventure was able to explain the relationship between the creator and the created.

> For Bonaventure, like Anselm is a mystic, and his attitude
> to the whole problem of the relation between faith and
> knowledge may be summed up in the words of the Prophet
> Isaiah, 'Nisi credideritis non intelligetis'. All perfect
> knowledge is dependent upon illumination... (Harris, 1927,
> p. 61)

In this, every creature was a mediated symbol of the divine. Every flower, every person, provides the subjective experience of the divine. God is not the flower, God touches our being through these creations.

It is Duns Scotus who truly solidifies the Franciscan understanding of Philosophy, mission and evangelization. John Duns Scotus, the Subtle Doctor, took the mysticism of Francis and Bonaventure and brought it to its Christocentric high point. In a simple and most profound form, Scotus states, God, so he taught, is love. Not only the source of love, but love, loving love in ultimate love itself. (Scotus, 1299, trans. 1966, p. 148) .

In defining the Franciscan program philosophically, Scotus makes this statement that reinterprets the very face of all creation. Thought itself, in so far as it is ordered by the will, is love. Scotus sees in the act of love both a freedom and immutability. All reality is love (Scotus, 1299, trans. 1966, Gemelli, 1935). By means of this statement, the secular and sacred division is healed. The cloister, protection against the wickedness of the world, vanishes.

This understanding that Franciscan mysticism could be transformed into a theology, helped to shape investigation into the natural world. Scientific observation and discovery by men such as Roger Bacon meant that investigating the world helped to reveal God more intimately. (Harris, 1927) In the same way, Raymond Lull investigated math and realistic logic. Yet, both of these men and their followers in the Franciscan school saw these investigations as means of evangelization.

In reference to Raymond Lull, Gemelli (1935) writes, "Like Bacon, he, too, sought out the truth solely for the purpose of defending and spreading the faith" (p. 63) But, even here, the Franciscan acknowledgment of the mediated language comes into play: "So, too, fully conscious that truths are brought home to men more easily by means of art than philosophy, he wrote three prose romances: *Blaquerna, Felix* and *Libre de Cavalleria*" (Gemelli, 1935, p. 63, [italics his]) .

In every manner conceivable Franciscans attempted to arrive at truth. Contrary to the popularly held belief that there is a tension between science and religion that Franciscans felt the sciences were simply another way to find God. Education and evangelization both lead forward in search of the eternal truth. Our continued struggle to construct learning about our environment and relationships moves us forward in understanding the divine plan.

This philosophical basis leads the Franciscan program into its popular tendencies. God can be found by humans through investigation into the world around them, through relationship with these created things, with beauty, science, math, logic, and others. This philosophy, based upon the mystical poetry of the *Canticle of the Creatures* will lead to popular devotions, a love for art, music, oration and education, and to political and theological movements. Intimacy with all creation will help to highlight injustice and form the basis for political upheaval and the formulation of theologies of liberation.

In the thirteenth century, St. Anthony with his popular preaching, imagery, and the use of animal and nature images that won people over to listen to his sermons. This famous preacher also represents another sector in the diverse program of Franciscan evangelization, scholarly pursuit. Francis is originally wary of intellectual pursuits, concerned that they may extinguish prayer. This is the same concern he shows for work (Francis of Assisi, 1223). However, once addressed, Francis bestows his blessing upon Anthony and those who follow in the scholarly tradition.

The mendicant entry into the academy was not always welcome by the older and more established orders. The history of the Universities of Paris and Cambridge are replete with the battles between the mendicants and the Benedictines. Yet, with the new Orders come new influences on philosophy, science and theology.

The Franciscan theology of love allows for a more generous view of human goodness. In the most popular statement of Scotus' philosophy, Christ is not incarnated simply to redeem humanity; even if there were no sin, he would have come out of love. Since Christ took on everything but sin, everything except sin will lead us to greater humanity and divinity.

If the world is a place for God's love to become manifest, the distinctions between the sacred and secular blur. This lessening of the distinction allows for far more breadth in experiencing God. No mere Pantheist, Francis sees the "footprints" of God in all creation, without exception. This philosophy of love allows for interplay in all realms to bring greater meaning and purpose to life.

Practical and Popular

The philosophical tradition of the Franciscans allowed for diversity. From this diverse philosophical tradition, popular piety emerged. The humanist tendencies of Franciscan spirituality called the friars into relationship with people.

> Instead of encouraging men to live in isolation and retirement, it (the Franciscan Spirit [emphasis mine]) sent them down into the squares and markets-places where the hard-working townsfolk had little need of being spurred to action, but rather of being taught to meditate and pray. The Franciscan sang like a jester, talked like a minstrel, and fought like a paladin of the Cross... (Gemelli, 1935, p. 44)

In the urban setting, Franciscans began to reach out using every form of expression known to humans. Friars preached in a simple, direct, and popular form. Stories and songs from the troubadour tradition and the nature mystics were adopted. By the 1400's friar preachers were joking, laughing, and even singing in the pulpit, a style that is still less accepted outside of the Franciscan sphere. The tragic death of Fr. Mychal Judge on September 11, 2001 and his subsequent funeral testified to this. Even TV commentators noted the differing tone of the ceremonies taking place in funerals at St. Patrick's Cathedral and that of the friars gathered at St. Francis, 31st Street for Fr. Mychal.

Popular piety was a tool for the Franciscans. Books were expensive and owned only by the few very wealthy citizens or the Church. The use of Latin in scripture and Church writings, known only to the learned of the time, prohibited access to these teachings by the common folk. Even if written in the vernacular, Biblical stories were incomprehensible to the common people who were illiterate. In order to bring the Gospel stories to the ordinary people the Franciscan adopted the educational methods of his day. The troubadour's melodies, which had told of wars and history, now carried Gospel lyrics. Sacred songs were composed in the vernacular and in a common musical style rather than in monastic chant. The most famous examples of these songs are Christmas carols, the development of which is credited to St. Francis.

Devotions also extended the experiences of monks and crusaders to all people. While field workers were not able to stop and go to church every three hours, the Angelus provided a means to consecrate each day for the common people. The Stations of the Cross provided people throughout the world the opportunity to join the journey of the passion of Christ in Jerusalem without joining the crusade. The Holy Name of Jesus could be preached as a pious observance or lifted as a battle standard. In each case, these devotions helped to move people to a more advanced understanding of their faith.

Devotion to the Holy Name of Jesus, the Stations of the Cross, processions, and the use of art and literature allowed Franciscans to reach out to all strata of people. Popular devotions were adaptable to the situation and applicable as necessary. Each of these devotions integrated the religious imagery, the language, the stories, and the tunes of the locale with the Gospel message in a way that made sense. People gained proximity to the Gospel through these forms.

Art and Literature

As parts of culture, art and literature hold a high place. Franciscan art emphasized simpler forms. Frescoes were used in place of marble relieves in many Franciscan churches during the Renaissance. Figures and motifs came to emphasize the joy and beauty of God.

> ...but in art and architecture too, hell began to recede into the distance and paradise to be placed in the foreground, the Crucified, with words of pardon on his lips, to be represented more frequently than Christ, as judge of the universe; while the Mother of God came down from her throne studded with precious jewels, and bent gently over her Babe, smiling at him as he lay on the straw of the manger. (Gemelli, 1935, p. 80)

Gemelli (1935) credits the Franciscans with the return of real life to art, as seen with Giotto. This return to real life is not the exclusive domain of art. Franciscan churches attempted to humanize the scale and form of worship by replacing longer liturgical chant with livelier and simpler melodies. The Franciscan rule (Francis of Assisi, 1223, trans. 1973) calls for breviaries to be carried by the clerics rather than the voluminous psalters of the monasteries. The stories of faith, whether the ancient stories of indigenous ancestors or scriptural stories, made use of the images and words known to local communities. It is that perspective, the human perspective, which is the most consistent factor in Franciscan philosophy, art, music, and literature. Ordinary expression of the common life is made holy.

Stories, in every sense, bring a new level of divinity to the human spirit. Whether it be the story told in common language, the story seen in art, or architecture, or music, or theater, the common element in Franciscan storytelling is the use of the vernacular or popular form. The reader may see in the Roman Church an acceptance of this idea with the movement from the Latin language to the vernacular or the simplification of artistic forms and rituals within the Church (Abbott, 1966). However, in all of these things, a Church vocabulary in art, music and symbol still reigns. The Franciscan mission has been to bring this language to the common person and to apply the language of the common person to the mission.

The history of the Franciscan order is marked by the humanization of all cultural elements. The cultural interplay of art, politics, music, and religion is viewed in terms of its impact on the common person. It is the duty of the Franciscan evangelizer to correlate that, which is present in a culture with the elements that are consistent with the Gospel. It is also his or her task to listen to and learn the language of the culture in order to inject Gospel values into the language. Education has precisely the same task, to bring new learning to individuals using whatever methods and symbols are most relevant and authentic for them.

The respect for individuality makes the Franciscan program unique. Rather than adopting program suited for all people, hearing one message, in one way, the Franciscan is called to develop an individualized evangelization plan for each person.

Politics plays an enormous role in education. The priorities of business and industry, the effects of cultural change from agriculture to information, the signs and symbols that are used to communicate realities are all cultural expressions. No educator in the United States, public or private would negate the impact of the political agenda on educational processes. Political platforms are built in many cases on education issues. School vouchers, standards, international competition, all impact the way education is provided in formal and less formal situations. The recent debate in the United States over funding for the National Endowment for the Arts shows the interplay of politics and cultural-educational expressions. The state, reflecting the perceived majority opinion, may move to limit the type of expression or education provided with state funds because of the "inappropriate" subject matter of the work.

In a similar way evangelization has been tied to politics. In the days of church-state unity, this meant that politics and religion were intertwined for a cultural whole. A heretical artistic expression or the teaching of heresy could end in imprisonment for subversion of the public good. Education was Church run through most of history, responsible for the promotion of both God and country.

The separation of church and state, a recent phenomenon in the history of the world, brings two major developments, neither directly causative, but at least correlative and especially evident in the United Sates. The first is that of compulsory education. A minimum universal standard is set for the entire country. Every citizen is required to attend school. This is a major cultural-educational shift that is still not evident in every culture or nation and which shows the clear linkages of culture, politics, and education.

The second is freedom of religion. Evangelization often meant converting the leader of a nation to a particular religion. With Church-state separation and freedom of religion, individuals or groups had to be convinced of the efficacy and benefits of a particular faith: again, a norm that is not universal throughout the world at the end of the twentieth century.

The movements in education and religion that struggle with these political-educational-cultural-religious issues are legion: Jewish schools, Mennonite and Amish communities, Fundamentalist Christians, Quakers, and Catholic schools. It is apparent that culture and politics, while not addressing an entirely new field of study, are an important part of the evangelization and education discussion.

Mission

St. Francis was not ecumenical in today's sense. For centuries, heresy was the worst abomination possible. Francis prescribed imprisonment for those friars who fell into this vile transgression (Francis of Assisi, 1226, trans. 1973). His first missions to Muslim lands were filled with zeal for bringing Christ's Good News to the infidels, even if it meant death, for which he hoped (Bonaventure, 1509, trans. 1973; Celano, 1229, trans. 1973). Yet, throughout the centuries, the Franciscans, maintaining the zeal of Francis, attempted dialogue, the most fundamental of ecumenical forms.

> The brothers who go can conduct themselves among them spiritually in two ways. One way is to avoid quarrels or disputes and *be subject to every human creature for God's sake* [italics his] (1 Pet. 2:13), so bearing witness to the fact that they are Christians. Another way is to proclaim the word of God openly, when they see that is God's will, calling on their hearers to believe in God almighty, father, Son, and Holy Spirit, the Creator of all, and in the Son, the Redeemer and Savior, that they may be baptized and become Christians. (Francis of Assisi, 1221, trans. 1973, p. 43)

St. Francis' first journey to the Holy Land was part of a crusade to meet the Sultan. His method was to speak with the leader and explain the goodness of God (St. Bonaventure, 1509, trans. 1973; Celano,

1229, trans. 1973). Similarly in the Franciscan debates with the (then considered heretical) followers of Zwingly; learning each other's language was an important step in searching for the truth. As the Rule of 1221 implies, the friar must assess the hearer's development in order to gauge the mode in which the Gospel would be preached, whether by example or word. Gemelli (1935) gives examples of a sixteenth century friars who were sent into areas of heresy in order to "win back" the faithful. He mentions one friar, John Wild:

> Not to destroy, but to build up; not to abandon scenes of
> difficulty, but to attempt to improve conditions; not to be
> terrified by the appearance of heresy, but to believe that, as
> God has permitted it, He will bring good out of evil--as, for
> instance, the awakening of drowsy pastors of souls: these
> were the principles on which John Wild acted. When
> brought into contact with the flame of love, heresy began to
> lose something of its venom. (p. 123)

The Franciscan mission continued this dialogue with believers other than Catholic and with cultures other than European. In the late 1700's Franciscans in China celebrated masses on portable altars and dressed in local garb and in Cairo translated the Pentateuch into Arabic (Gemelli, 1935). In the Americas, the Franciscans intermingled the customs of the indigenous with those of Christians. Today, in the Guatemalan villages of Chichicastenago and San Andres syncretistic celebrations of Christianity and ancient pagan symbols are intermingled.

Politics and Cultural Symbols

Evangelization was not often separated from politics. Franciscan history bears this out. The very essence of Franciscan poverty put the friars (minori) at odds with the wealthy (majori). The focus against materialism and the acquisition of possessions is a political theme to this day. By rejecting the trappings of the mercantile class, the friars were situated firmly among the poor.

In the early rule of the Third Order of St. Francis (1226, trans. 1973, p. 171) followers were forbidden to take feudal oaths or carry weapons, adding a significant and practical dimension to the language of the Gospel. During the conquest of the New World, the Franciscan presence was as much political as religious, carrying the needs of the crown sometimes in place of the cross. The great dialogue that took place with much of the world, whether Arab or indigenous American, came on the wake of the sword. The positive and negative effects of this mixture of cultural elements were present.

More recently, the birth of liberation theology (Gutierrez, 1973; Sobrino, 1985; Boff, 1986), most significantly that of Friar Leonardo Boff, has attempted to explain this interplay of the political and religious struggle. It is the Franciscan propensity for the human struggle that makes the friars more readily accepting of syncretization of every cultural element. It is also the proximity to the human struggle, which makes human injustice more obvious to the friars. The justice dimensions of the Gospel are constitutive, not only theologically, but also practically, because it involves those people or creatures with whom friars are in relationship.

These examples, historic and current, illustrate the close connections among culture and evangelization. Whether in artistic representations or political struggles, theology is expressed in terms of relationship and response.

The Franciscans' radical understanding that God is love and that creation reflects God's love provides for a positive initial dialogue with all people and religions. The prescription of the Rule of Francis (1221) reflects the need to establish the baseline for Franciscan evangelization first, so that the friars may then, according to God's will, determine the best method by which to proceed. Both the rule and the stories of Francis' walking through the streets as a means of preaching (Celano, 1229, trans. 1973) attest to the importance of modeling as a means of testimony to God's goodness.

The apostolic colleges of the sixteenth century in America and the missions of Juniper Serra followed the same custom of establishing a base community from which to move. I acknowledge that the mission establishment brought death, destruction and slavery to of the indigenous population. Much of this was because of the governmental connection with missionary activity common to the time. The establishment of the Spanish missions in the United States was governmental and religious. This is a concept that seems foreign to those reared in the age of Church-State separation. However, it was the intention of the missionaries to bring what they believed was good to the region. Schools and hospitals were among the first establishments of the friars. In this, they brought not only the Gospel, but also practical applications for the well being of native Americans.

In each region, the friars would set up a house as a station from which to send and receive friars. At any one time in the Antigua, Guatemala college, for instance, one hundred friars would be going out, one hundred friars returning, and one hundred friars preparing for the next trip. The formation for mission was not only theological; it included the telling of stories. Upon the return of each mission trip, the friars would gather in chapter and share the tales of their journeys, their successes and struggles (Gemelli, 1935). The customs and languages of the Americas were passed on through these colleges.

Establishing base communities was the pattern for Asia, the Americas, and the Middle East, and in recent mission efforts in Africa. In each case, the understanding that living in peace with people and without dispute is the basic tenet. This living situation also allows friars to examine the cultural elements of the environment in which they find themselves. A baseline for evangelization depends upon the stories, symbols, and other cultural supports that are already present. Rejecting what is contrary to the Gospel and accepting what is supportive of the Gospel is discerned in the day-to-day life of the friars living among the people of the area.

Love, as the basis of evangelization, seems simplistic. However, history shows that love has not always been the motivating principle for mission or evangelization. The Franciscan philosophical basis provides room for diverse understandings. While Francis and the Order have always insisted upon absolute orthodoxy and allegiance to the Pope (Francis, 1221) , the mission and evangelization program has also insisted upon experience and relationship as discernment criteria.

An example of this discernment from relationship comes from my experience in Guatemala. Local witchcraft traditions are obviously not in line with the Gospel. Yet, the Franciscans have not banned witches from performing rites within the churches, making use of holy water and images, but have learned about candle colors and blessings. While a white candle asks a blessing upon a child and a yellow a blessing upon an adult, a black candle asks for a curse. It is the burning of black candles that is forbidden within the Franciscan churches. This toleration for blessings, mixing that which is within the indigenous tradition with that which is doctrinally Catholic, comes from an understanding of culture and a relationship with people. To deny the burning of candles would be to alienate people completely from the church, a stance taken by other orders and sects.

There is a necessity in evangelization today to accept individuals where in their moment and place in history. Making use of the symbols and signs that can help them to construct meaning in their lives, the Church uses a variety of modes. The implications of culture and education in this process are readily apparent. Education also makes use of these signs and symbols in bringing a person forward in understanding. The use of educational concepts and expressions may help to communicate the program of evangelization. Assessment of people in terms of their social and proximal development, assessing language to identify status, listening to stories to understand what new elements can be added to advance the person to a greater state are all educational techniques that can be used by Franciscan evangelists.

References

Abbott, W. (Ed.). (1966). *The documents of Vatican II.* New York: America Press.

Anderson, W. T. (Ed.). (1995). *The truth about the truth: De-confusing and re-constructing the postmodern world.* New York: G.P. Putnam's Sons.

Bauer, R. A., & Carper, J. C. (1998). Spirituality and the public schools: An evangelical perspective. *Educational Leadership, 56,* 33-37.

Bettoni, E. (1959). *Nothing for your journey.* Chicago: Franciscan Herald Press.

Blanck, G. (1990). Vygotsky: The man and his cause. In L. Moll (Ed.), (1990). In L. C. Moll (Ed.), *Vygotsky and education: Instructional implications and applications of sociohistorical psychology.* New York: The Cambridge University Press.

Boff, L. (1986). *Liberation theology: from dialogue to confrontation.* New York: Harper & Row.

Bonaventure, (trans.1973). Major life of St. Francis. In M. Habig (Ed.) , *St. Francis of Assisi: omnibus of sources.* Chicago, IL: Franciscan Herald Press.

Brown, A. L. and Ferrara, R. A. (1985). Diagnosing zones of proximal development. In J. Wertsch (Ed.), *Culture, communication and cognition: Vygotskian perspectives.* Cambridge: Cambridge University Press.

Bruner, J. S. (1973). *Beyond the information given.* New York: W. W. Norton & Co.

Bruner, J. S. (1996). *The culture of education.* Cambridge, MA: Harvard University Press.

Burghardt, W. (1987 . *Preaching: the art and the craft.* New York: Paulist Press.

Carozzo, A. (1984, May/June). The mission to preach: A Franciscan perspective. *Review for religious, 43,* 444-453.

Celano, Thomas of . (trans. 1973) . First life of St. Francis. In M. Habig (Ed.), *St. Francis of Assisi: Omnibus of sources.* Chicago, IL: Franciscan Herald Press.

Clinchy, E. (1995). Learning in and about the real world: Recontextualizing public schooling. *Phi Delta Kappan, 76* (5), 400-404.

Clay, M. M. & Courtney, B. C. (1990). A Vygotskian interpretation of reading recovery. In L. C. Moll (Ed.), *Vygotsky and education: Instructional implications and applications of sociohistorical psychology.* New York: The Cambridge University Press.

Codex Iuris Canonica. (1983). Vatican City: Libreria Editrice Vaticana.

Cole, Michael (1985) . The zone of proximal development: where culture and cognition create each other. In J. Wertsch (Ed.), *Culture, communication and cognition: Vygotskian perspectives.* Cambridge: Cambridge University Press.

Cole, Michael (1996). *Cultural psychology.* Cambridge, MA: Harvard University Press.

Congregation for the Doctrine of the Faith. (2000). *On the unicity and universal salvation of Jesus Christ and the Church.* Boston: Pauline Books and Media.

Davare, D. W. (1994). An explanation of shared programs. *PSBA Bulletin, 4* (5), 8-9.

Donohue, J. W. (1997). The book much read. *America, 176,* 26-29.

Diaz, R. D. , Neal , C. J. & Amaya-Williams, M. The social origins of self-regulation. (1990). In L.C. Moll (Ed.), *Vygotsky and education: Instructional implications and applications of sociohistorical psychology.* New York: The Cambridge University Press.

Diocese of Pittsburgh. (January 1998). *A Planning guide for the reaccredidation of total quality Catholic schools in the diocese of Pittsburgh.* Pittsburgh, PA .

Donahue, J. W. , (1967). Education, Articles on. In *The new Catholic encyclopedia* (Vol. 5, p. 111) . New York: McGraw-Hill.

Eagan, J. (1995). *Restoration and renewal.* Kansas City: Sheed and Ward.

Education Leadership, 56 (4).

Forman ,E. A. & Cazden, C. B. Exploring Vygotskian perspectives in education: the cognitive value of peer interaction. . In J. Wertsch (Ed.), *Culture, communicationand cognition: Vygotskian perspectives.* Cambridge: Cambridge University Press.

Francis of Assisi, (trans. 1973). The Rule of 1221. In M. Habig (Ed.), *St. Francis of Assisi: Omnibus of sources* (pp. 168-175) . Chicago, IL: Franciscan Herald Press. .

Francis of Assisi, (trans. 1973). First rule of the third order. In M. Habig (Ed.), *St. Francis of Assisi: Omnibus of sources* (pp. 168-175). Chicago, IL: Franciscan Herald Press.

Francis of Assisi, (trans. 1973). The Rule of 1223. In M. Habig (Ed.), *St. Francis of Assisi: Omnibus of sources* (pp. 57-66). Chicago, IL: Franciscan Herald Press.

Francis of Assisi, (trans. 1973). The Testament. In M. Habig (Ed.), *St. Francis of Assisi: Omnibus of sources* (pp. 67-70). Chicago, IL: Franciscan Herald Press.

The Gallup Poll: Religious faith is widespread but many skip church: 1997. [On-line] Princeton, NJ: The Gallup Organization.

Gallimore, R. & Tharp, R. (1990). Teaching mind in society: Teaching, schooling, and literate discourse. In L. C . Moll (Ed.), *Vygotsky and education: Instructional implications and applications of sociohistorical psychology.* New York: The Cambridge University Press.

Gardner, H. (1982). *Developmental psychology* (second edition) Boston: Little, Brown and Company.

Gemelli, A. (1935). *The Franciscan message to the world.* (H. L. Hughes, Trans.). London: Burns, Oates &Washbourne, Ltd.

Ginsburg, C. (1976). *The cheese and the worms.* New York: Penguin Books.

Goble, N. (1993). New realities of effective school-community relations. *PSBA Bulletin 57,* (4) , 8-12.

Griffin, J. (1991). Reflections on evangelization yesterday, today and tomorrow. *Origins, 21* (4), 57-66.

Gutierrez, Gustavo. (1973). *A theology of liberation.* New York: Orbis Books.

Harris, C. R. S. (1927). *Duns Scotus.* Oxford: Clarendon Press.

Harris, X. J. , (1967). Education, Articles on. In *The new Catholic encyclopedia* (Vol. 5, p.138). New York: McGraw-Hill.

Hedegaard, M. (1990). The zones of proximal development as basis for instruction. In L. C. Moll (Ed.), *Vygotsky and education: Instructional implications and applications of sociohistorical psychology.* New York: The Cambridge University Press.

Heft, J. (1998). *Reflections on Catholic education.* An address given to the Catholic school principals of the diocese. Pittsburgh, PA.

Interdicasterial Commission for the Catechism of the Catholic Church.(1994). *The catechism of the Catholic Church.* Rome: Libreria Editrice Vaticana.

International Commission for English in the Liturgy. (1972). *The rites of the Catholic Church as revised by the second Vatican ecumenical council.* New York: Pueblo.

Jones, M. (Nov. 1994). An interview with Camille Paglia. *America, 171,* 2,10-12.

John Paul II. (1990). *Redemptoris missio.* Church documents: Conciliar and post-conciliar. (Windows) [Computer software]. Boston, MA: Daughters of St. Paul.

Johnson, T.(1995, January/February). Back to the future: Franciscan literary tradition, virtual reality, and infomania. *Review for religious, 54,* 22-40.

Kennedy, L. (1995). *Susan Sontag: Mind as passion.* New York: Manchester University Press.

Kung, H. (1978). *Does God exist?* New York: Crossroad.

Kung, H. (1988). *Theology for the third millenium.* New York: Doubleday.

Kung, H. (1991). *Paradigm change in theology.* New York: Crossroad.

Lee, B. (1985). Intellectual origins of Vygotsky's semiotic analysis. In J. Wertsch (Ed.), *Culture, communication and cognition:Vygotskian perspectives.* Cambridge: Cambridge University Press.

Legend of the three companions (1244?). In M. Habig (Ed.), *St. Francis of Assisi: Omnibus of sources.* (pp. 853-954). Chicago, IL: Franciscan Herald Press.

Luria, A. R. (1982). *Language and cognition.* New York: John Wiley & Sons.

McCown, R., Driscoll, M., & Roop, P. (1996). *Educational psychology* (second edition). Boston: Allyn & Bacon.

McLaughlin, J. (1993, March/April). The meaning of evangelization today. *Review for religious, 52,* 194-201.

McNamee, G. D. (1990). Learning to read and write in an inner-city setting: A longitudinal study of community change. In L. C. Moll (Ed.), *Vygotsky and education: Instructional implications and applications of sociohistorical psychology.* New York: The Cambridge University Press.

Moll, L. C. & Greenberg, J. B. (1990). Creating zones of proximal development. In L. C. Moll (Ed.), *Vygotsky and education: Instructional implications and applications of sociohistorical psychology.* New York: The Cambridge University Press.

Moll, L. C. (Ed.), (1990). *Vygotsky and education: Instructional implications and applications of sociohistorical psychology.* New York: The Cambridge University Press.

Reese, T. (1997, June 21-28). 2001 and Beyond: Preparing the Church for the Next Millennium. *America, 176,* 10-18.

Reeves, T. (1996). *The empty church.* New York: Touchstone.

Scotus, J. D. (trans. 1966). *A treatise on God as the first principle.* Chicago, IL: Franciscan Herald Press.

Schaluck, H., Carraro, F. R. , De Nunzio E. , Serrini, L. Quilis, J.A. and Echavarren, M. E. (1995). *Anthony man of the Gospel: Letter of the ministers general of the Franciscan family.* Pulaski, Wisconsin: Franciscan Publishers.

Schaluck, H., (1996) . *To fill the whole world with the gospel of Christ.* St. Louis: English Speaking Conference.

Schaluck, H. (1997). *Report to the general chapter.* Rome: General Curia of the Friars Minors.

Scribner, S. (1985). Vygotsky's uses of history. In J. Wertsch (Ed.), *Culture, communication and cognition: Vygotskian perspectives.* Cambridge: Cambridge University Press.

Scribner, S. (1997). Knowledge at work . In E. Tobach, R. J. Falmagne, M. B. Parlee, L. M. W. Martin and A. S. Kapelman (Eds.), *Mind and social practice.* New York: The Cambridge University Press.

Scribner, S. (1997). A sociocultural approach to the study of mind. In E. Tobach, R. J. Falmagne, M. B. Parlee, L. M. W. Martin and A. S. Kapelman (Eds.), *Mind and social practice.* New York: The Cambridge University Press.

Scribner, S. (1997). Vygotsky's uses of history. In E. Tobach, R. J. Falmagne, M. B. Parlee, L. M. W. Martin and A. S. Kapelman (Eds.), *Mind and social practice.* New York: The Cambridge University Press.

Shank, G. (1994), Shaping qualitative research in educational psychology. *Contemporary Educational Psychology, 19,* 340-359.

Shank, G. (1998). The extraordinary ordinary powers of abductive reasoning. *Theory & Psychology, 8,* (6): 841-860.

Smith, H. (1995). Postmodernism and the world's religions. In W. Anderson (Ed.), *The truth about truth: De-confusing and reconstructing the postmodern world.* New York: G. P. Putnam's Sons.

Sobrino, J. (1985). *Theology of Christian solidarity.* New York: Orbis.

Sontag, S. (1963). *The benefactor.* New York: Anchor Books Doubleday.

Sontag, S. (1966). *Styles of radical will.* New York: Anchor Books Doubleday.

Sontag, S. (1967). *Death kit.* New York: Anchor Books Doubleday.

Sontag, S. (1972). *Under the sign of Saturn.* New York: Anchor Books Doubleday.

Sontag, S. (1973). *On photography.* New York: Anchor Books Doubleday.

Sontag, S. (Winter, 1995). The art of fiction. *The Paris review, 137.* (pp. 177-208)

Sontag, S. & Hodgkin, H., (1987). *The way we live now.* New York: The Noonday Press.

Szoka, E. (1989), The unchurched and the use of the mass media for evangelization. *Origins, 18,* 720-721.

Thompson,S. (1995), The community as classroom. *Educational leadership, 52* (8), 17-20.

Tracy, D. (1994). *On naming the present: God, hermeneutics, and church.* New York: Orbis.

Tudge, J. (1990). Vygotsky, the zone of proximal development, and peer collaboration: Implications for classroom practice. In L. Moll (Ed.), *Vygotsky and education: Instructional implications and applications of sociohistorical psychology.* New York: The Cambridge University Press.

Valsiner, J. [ed.] (1989). *Child development in cultural context.* Toronto: Hogrefe and Huber Publishers.

Vygotsky, L. S. (1978). *Mind in society.* Cambridge: Harvard University Press.

Vygotsky, L. S. (1986). *Thought and language.* (A. Kozulin, Ed. & Trans.). Cambridge, MA: The MIT Press.

Vygotsky, L. S. (1997). *Educational psychology.* (R. Silverman, Trans.). Boca Raton, FL: St. Lucie Press.

Vygotsky, L.S. and Luria, A.R. (1998). *Studies on the history of primitive behavior: ape, primitive, and child.* (V. I. Golod & J.E. Know, Trans.). Hillsdale, New Jersey: Lawrence Erlbaum Associates.

Wertsch, J. V. (1990). The voice of rationality in a sociocultural approach to mind. In L. Moll (Ed.), *Vygotsky and education: Instructional implications and applications of sociohistorical psychology.* New York: The Cambridge University Press.

Wertsch, J. V. (1991). *Voices of the mind.* Cambridge, MA: Harvard University Press.

Wertsch, J. V. (1998). *Mind as action.* New York: Oxford University Press.

Index

About the Author

Michael Ledoux is a member of the Order of Friars Minor (Franciscans). He is the holder of the Sisters of Saint Francis Endowed Chair in Franciscan Studies and an Associate Professor of Education at Neumann College. An educator for more than twenty years, Michael served as both an elementary and high school principal. He served as an adjunct professor at Duquesne University and continues as an on-line consultant for the Teaching as Intentional Learning Program for Center for the Advancement of Teaching and Learning (CASTL) at that institution.

In addition to teaching, Michael has served as a friar priest in Guatemala, El Salvador and Honduras. He has also worked as a lobbyist and advocate nationally and internationally for issues of justice and peace, representing the Conference of Major Superiors of Men, USA.

Michael will begin as Vice President for University Ministries at St. Bonaventure University in the 2002-2003 academic year.